The Place of Joy

Finding Joy and Meaning in Life in the 21st Century

Strat Goodhue

First Call Publishing

Bellevue, Washington

The Place of Joy

Finding Joy and Meaning in Life in the 21st Century

Contents

14- WHAT A VIEW! 221

ACKNOWLEDGMENTS

Of course, first and foremost I am thankful to God. It has been such a blessing writing and working on this book, knowing that God can use even me, to bless people. It is a privilege I could never deserve. I started writing this book with the conviction that many Christians are not living the lives of joy that God wants them to live. As I prayed, studied and wrote, I realized that as I was putting together the message I believe God wanted me to share with others, He was changing my life and filling me with joy as well. I am so blessed.

I am also grateful for my wonderful wife, Doreen. She is such a blessing. She not only helped make this a better book; she is a useful tool in the Lord's hands to help me live a life of joy.

I want to express my special appreciation for my brothers and sisters in Christ with whom I share prayer requests. I'm sure their prayers and encouragement are more valuable than they or I know.

I am also grateful for the editing help given by my brothers and sister in Christ- Garry Bishop, Barbara Gillis, Tim Newman, Dennis Robertson, Tracy Tyson and Troy Zinszer.

I would like to express my deep gratitude for Pastor Tim and Kathy Newman, Charlie Cook, and many others whose prayers, encouragement and support for Doreen and I have been such a big part of this book being written.

Lastly, I offer my sincere appreciation to those of you who will read this book and I pray, as a result, live lives that are more full of joy.

Introduction

**"And these things we write to you
that your joy may be full."**

- 1 John 1:4

Jesus only had a few hours to live before He was crucified. In His final message before going to the cross, He shared His heart with His disciples. He talked about our relationship with God and then He said, "These things I have spoken to you, that My joy may remain in you, and that your joy may be full."[1] So why, in Jesus' final message before His death, was He telling us about our relationship with God? As He said, it's because He wants us to have fullness of joy. Obviously, us having fullness of joy, is important to Jesus.

What if I told you that I can guarantee you a life of joy? Would you think it sounds too good to be true? The truth is that God doesn't want us to get through this life as mere survivors- people who just make it to the end in spite of all the difficulties along the way. There's more to life- a lot more. And a lot of people are missing out on the joy God wants to give us.

There seems to be a part of me that thinks I shouldn't live a life of joy. Am I the only one that thinks this way? The thought comes to mind that I really don't deserve to live "the good life." Do you ever think like that? "I deserve some good things in life, but I don't really deserve to live a life filled with joy." Well, you know what? That's right. You and I aren't perfect. We don't deserve to live a life filled with joy. But God wants to give us that life anyway- because He loves us.

---

[1] John 15:11

Does God want you to be rich beyond your wildest dreams, to be married to Mr. or Mrs. Perfect and to live on a tropical island paradise, sipping coconut drinks all day? No, but He wants you to live a life full of rich joy, wonderful peace and deep contentment, regardless of what you have been through, are going through, or will go through in life. In the pages of this book, you will discover how to find joy, how to keep it, and how to live that life of joy, peace and deep contentment that we all long for. You will also discover how to finish strong- how to live life in such a way that you can look back and know you have lived your life to the fullest- that you have lived a life of meaning and significance, and that you have lived a life that has pleased God.

It's been said that the ultimate goal of all human endeavor is to find happiness. People try all kinds of things to find it. Many people think they will be happy if they have a lot of material possessions. They strive for years to attain the standard of living they think will provide happiness, but they are never able to attain it. The economy takes a turn for the worse. That investment just doesn't pan out like they hoped it would, or health or other problems get in the way of reaching their goals. They settle for a life of mediocrity- "Oh well, it could be worse."

Other people work for years to get those things they think will bring them financial independence and a life of ease and happiness and after years of striving, they are able to attain them, but then they find they are too old, too busy, or too sick to enjoy what they've worked so hard for. Others find that wealth really just brings them emptiness and doesn't result in the joy they were seeking.

Some people think happiness can be found in good health, beauty or fame, or that happiness comes from being kind or honest. Some think happiness comes from a combination of the above.

The truth is that anyone who hungers for true joy and contentment will only find it in God. Every other pursuit in the quest for joy is chasing shadows, and the pursuit of a shadow will never bring real, lasting joy. The joy we all desire- true, deep, satisfying joy, can only be found in God. As A.W. Tozer said, "Trying to be happy without God's presence is like trying to have a bright day without the sun." If we want to live extraordinary lives, lives that are filled with rich joy and deep contentment, we need to learn how to have an extraordinary relationship with God- and it's simple to do.

Augustine (a theologian who lived in the fourth century) said, "... our heart is restless until it rests in God."[2] If this is true, what does it mean to have our hearts "rest in God"? How can we who live busy lives in the 21st century, somehow have our hearts rest in God? How can we go through trials and have our hearts rest in God? In this book, we will see what it means to truly rest in God, and how easy it is, regardless of our circumstances.

Are there some simple changes we can make in our lives that will result in our lives being transformed from ordinary to extraordinary? Yes, and the extraordinary life of peace and joy is available to every one of us. If you take the truths of this book to heart, it will change the way you think about Heaven, the way you think about yourself, your life, and probably even the way you think about God.

Opinions are a dime a dozen. The world is full of people who are more than willing to tell you what they think. But in the end, what people think doesn't really matter- what matters is what God thinks. And what God says. That's why this book is not a book of psychology or man's wisdom. This book looks at what the Creator of the universe says about something He says He wants to give all of us- joy. The Bible- God's Word, is absolutely true. That's why you can absolutely depend on what it says. And that's why it is quoted so many times in this book. Who really cares what I think- we want to know what God thinks.

---

[2] Augustinus: Confessiones 1,1

It doesn't matter if up to this point you've lived a life of poverty or affluence, ease or adversity, sickness or health; God wants you to live a life of joy and fulfillment. Jesus said He came to give us abundant life.[3] And He said, "These things I have spoken to you, that My joy may remain in you, and that your joy may be full."[4] We shouldn't feel guilty or fearful because we want to live a life of joy- God desires that every one of us live in fullness of joy.

What is happiness? What is joy? And how can we live a life of joy? Read on. Join me on a journey of joy.

---

[3] John 10:10
[4] John 15:11

1

What is Joy?

"The joy of the Lord is your strength."
- Nehemiah 8:10

Success Made Simple

There is a song that became popular for a time, titled, "Don't Worry, Be Happy." Wouldn't it be nice if it were that easy? If we could somehow just make the choice to always be happy? You just lost your spouse, your job, your health, a child or another family member, your home, your possessions, your life savings, your dreams, you have no place to live? "Don't worry. Be happy." The reality is that it doesn't work that way. When we are faced with the very real and sometimes extremely difficult situations in life, we can't just choose to "be happy" and not worry.

Even if we aren't experiencing difficulties, our lives can lack joy. John D. Rockefeller was the world's richest man and the first American to make a billion dollars. He is often regarded as the richest person in history.[1] It has been reported that after amassing a billion dollars, he was asked, "How much money is enough?" and that he answered, "Just a little bit more." Whether or not he really said that, it illustrates people's appetite for more. "If I just had more money." "If I just had her, or him." "If I just had more recognition or power." "If I was just over there." "If I just had more stuff." "If people would just appreciate me more." "If

---

[1] Adjusting for inflation.

only I was famous." "If only I was married." "If only I was single." How much is enough? What will it take to fill our lives with joy and satisfaction?

Ultimately, money, people, power, fame, recognition, houses, appreciation and stuff will not satisfy. The thrill of them may be an easy thing for us to imagine, and sometimes they can bring us temporary happiness, but the truth is that they won't really satisfy us. Even if we do experience temporary joy and contentment from these things; that's all it will be- temporary. I once heard a pastor joking about his age. He said, "I'm 54 years old. People keep telling me I'm middle-aged. I would feel a lot better about that if I knew more 108 year olds." I laughed at the joke, but then I thought, "Wait a minute. If Americans live about 80 years on average, and I'm 40, it means I am now middle-aged!" I went from being young, to being middle-aged, in the time it took that pastor to tell one joke!

> **What will it take to fill our lives with joy and satisfaction?**

I realize I didn't really get any older by him telling the joke, but it was the first time in my life that I realized I am now middle-aged (and that was over 10 years ago). (I'm now 55.) Life is so short. It seems like it was only a few years ago I was in the first grade, walking down the hallway in my elementary school, looking up at fourth graders, thinking about how old they looked. I keep adjusting in my mind what "old" is. I used to think it was 30, and then 40. As I got older, I decided, "No, 50 is when you are old." Now that I am 55, I'm thinking that 90 is actually when a person starts to get old.

Charlie

I am blessed by my friendship with Charlie. He loves the Lord and has a zeal for life. He radiates the joy of the Lord and wants to make his life count for eternity. Charlie hasn't reached retirement age yet. He still drives his car, works an almost full-time job and walks several times a week to stay in shape. Charlie is now 101 years old. (I want to be like Charlie when I grow up.) While he is pushing the boundaries of what many people think of as "old," at some point all of us will have to face the truth. As teenagers, it seems like our lives on this earth are going to last forever. But as those decades tick away, at some point reality strikes- life is short. As the Bible says, life is "a vapor that appears for a little time and then vanishes away."[2] Our life is like a puff of smoke. Have you ever watched the smoke rising up from a fire, or that comes out of a smoke stack? It's there for a moment or two, and then "poof," it's gone. That's what our lives are like. Life really is short and we should make the most of the little time we have.

The Cosmic Killjoy

You've probably heard people say things like, "I'm going to live for myself now, but in the future I'm going to give my life to God." A lot of people think God is a cosmic killjoy, sitting up in Heaven trying to figure out ways to make our lives miserable. When I first asked Jesus to come into my life and to forgive my sins, I thought my life would be stripped of its joy. I wondered if God was going to have me move to a foreign country as a missionary and marry a woman with a bone stuck through her nose. I don't mean to disrespect any foreign cultures (or anyone in the U.S. who sticks things through their nose), but as someone who was raised in the U.S. in the '60s and '70s, it just wasn't very appealing to me. I thought God would ask me to do the things I most hated to do. Why do we think like that? It's because we don't understand who God is. The God who created us and wants to guide our lives is the God whose plans for us are good.[3] The angels who announced the birth of Jesus, said, "I bring you good news of great joy which will be for all the people."[4] He said it's "good news of great joy." He wants us to rejoice with

---

[2] James 4:14
[3] Jeremiah 29:11
[4] Luke 2:10 (NASB)

"joy inexpressible."[5] There will be times (and sometimes those times will be seasons) when we can't understand why certain things are happening the way they are, but as we learn the secrets of living a life of joy, we can have joy, regardless of the circumstances.

Joy is not a secondary issue in life. As C.S. Lewis said, "Joy is the serious business of Heaven."[6] Most Christians are familiar with the word "grace." Grace is the undeserved kindness of God. It's one of the things that separate Christianity from all other religions. In other religions, rewards are all earned. The Bible teaches that God in His lovingkindness gives us what we don't deserve- grace. Grace is absolutely central to Christianity. And if grace is central; then joy is central. While most Christians are familiar with the concept of God's grace, many don't know that the word "grace" in the New Testament could be defined as "that which affords joy, pleasure, delight..."[7] It comes from the Greek root word which means "to joy, rejoice, be glad."[8] Joy is not just something we all want; it's at the heart of what God wants to give to us. He wants to give us grace- that which results in joy, pleasure and delight.

> The word "Grace" comes from the Greek root word which means "to joy, rejoice, be glad." Joy is not just something we all want; it's at the heart of what God wants to give to us.

Jesus and Joy

Some people think when Jesus was on the earth, He walked around with a scowl on His face. They think that is a sign of true "holiness." God came to this earth in human form in the person of Jesus Christ,[9] so we know that nobody who

---

[5] 1 Peter 1:8
[6] C.S. Lewis, Letters To Malcolm Chiefly On Prayer, 92-93
[7] Thayer's Lexicon
[8] Vine's Expository Dictionary of New Testament Words
[9] John 1:1; Philippians 2:5-8

has ever lived was more filled with the Holy Spirit than Jesus. And we know that along with love- the Holy Spirit produces joy.[10] So if you think of Jesus as being a man who was stern and serious all the time, you should rethink your beliefs about the character of Jesus. The psalmist prophesied about Jesus, saying, "God has anointed You with the oil of gladness more than Your companions."[11] Jesus was not a sourpuss. He was a man of joy and was "anointed with the oil of gladness."[12] Jesus even rebuked those who thought He was having too good a time with people.[13] We know of at least one occasion when Jesus "rejoiced greatly in the Holy Spirit."[14] He even commanded His followers to rejoice.[15] Jesus came to bring us the Kingdom of God, and as the Bible tells us- the Kingdom of God is "righteousness and peace and joy in the Holy Spirit."[16] Jesus was loving, peaceful, longsuffering, kind, good, faithful, gentle and self-controlled. Jesus was also- a man of joy.[17]

The famous preacher Jonathan Edwards said, "the religion of heaven consists chiefly in holy and mighty love and joy... "[18] A few of the things mentioned in the Bible about joy include, "But let all those rejoice who put their trust in You; Let them ever shout for joy."[19] "In Your presence is fullness of joy; At Your right hand are pleasures forevermore."[20] "...the joy of Your salvation."[21] "He brought out His people with joy,

---

[10] Galatians 5:22
[11] Psalm 45:7; Hebrews 1:9
[12] Isaiah 53:3-4 tells us He was "a man of sorrows and acquainted with grief" but that is referring to His crucifixion, not His general disposition.
[13] Matthew 11:18-19
[14] Luke 10:21 (NASB)
[15] Matthew 5:12; Luke 10:20
[16] Romans 14:17
[17] Galatians 5:22
[18] Religious Affections, pg. 22
[19] Psalm 5:11
[20] Psalm 16:11
[21] Psalm 51:12

His chosen ones with gladness."[22] "With joy you will draw water from the wells of salvation."[23] "The humble also shall increase their joy in the LORD,"[24] "I will joy in the God of my salvation."[25] "The kingdom of heaven is like treasure hidden in a field, which a man found and hid; and for joy over it he goes and sells all that he has and buys that field."[26] "His lord said to him, 'Well done, good and faithful servant; you were faithful over a few things, I will make you ruler over many things. Enter into the joy of your lord.'"[27]

"Then the angel said to them, "Do not be afraid, for behold, I bring you good tidings of great joy which will be to all people."[28] "There is joy in the presence of the angels of God over one sinner who repents."[29] "These things I have spoken to you, that My joy may remain in you, and that your joy may be full."[30] "Ask, and you will receive, that your joy may be full."[31] "But now I come to You, and these things I speak in the world, that they may have My joy fulfilled in themselves."[32] "the disciples were filled with joy and with the Holy Spirit."[33] "that I may finish my race with joy... "[34] "the kingdom of God is... righteousness and peace and joy in the Holy Spirit."[35] "may the God of hope fill you with all joy and peace in believing."[36] "we... are fellow workers for your joy."[37] "But the

---

[22] Psalm 105:43
[23] Isaiah 12:3
[24] Isaiah 29:19
[25] Habakkuk 3:18
[26] Matthew 13:44
[27] Matthew 25:21
[28] Luke 2:10
[29] Luke 15:10
[30] John 15:11
[31] John 16:24
[32] John 17:13
[33] Acts 13:52
[34] Acts 20:24
[35] Romans 4:17
[36] Romans 15:13

fruit of the Spirit is love, joy..."[38] "joy of faith."[39] "Jesus... who for the joy that was set before Him endured the cross... "[40] "And these things we write to you that your joy may be full."[41] "Now to Him who is able to keep you from stumbling, and to present you faultless before the presence of His glory with exceeding joy."[42]

It is very clear from these and many more verses in the Bible, that God is very "serious" about joy. When the Apostle Paul tells us, "the kingdom of God is... righteousness and peace and joy in the Holy Spirit,"[43] we can see that joy should be one of the central things in our lives. It should be a huge part of who we are. That's what the Kingdom of God is- "righteousness and peace and joy in the Holy Spirit."[44] Jesus said, "These things I have spoken to you, that My joy may remain in you, and that your joy may be full."[45] It is absolutely clear that God desires for us all to have fullness of joy.

What is Joy?

So what is joy? Is it different than happiness? You may have heard it said that happiness and joy are two different things. "Happiness depends on happenings," is a commonly expressed saying. This can be a useful way of remembering the difference between happiness and joy. While happiness depends on outward circumstances (the happenings); real joy, Biblical joy, is a deep, abiding sense of gladness. So joy is really an abiding sense of happiness. Even though there are times of disappointment, discouragement, sorrow or fear, a

---

[37] 2 Corinthians 1:24
[38] Galatians 5:22
[39] Philippians 1:25
[40] Hebrews 12:2
[41] 1 John 1:4
[42] Jude 1:24
[43] Romans 14:17
[44] Romans 14:17
[45] John 15:11

person with joy knows that even though they may be under a passing cloud, the sun is always shining up above the clouds, and they will see it again. Having joy even in trials can make all the difference in the world.

People who have joy smile a lot. They laugh. They tend to be optimistic and are able to make it through times of difficulties that would stop other people in their tracks. They see possibilities where others see roadblocks. Have you ever noticed how difficult it is to offend a truly joyful person? Insults can roll off a joyful person like water off a duck's back. Their joy is contagious and you feel bad when you dislike a joyful person. Joyful people have vitality and a zest for living.

Some people act as if they were baptized in lemon juice. They seem to be in a constantly sour mood. When I was a little boy, there was a cartoon on television called Gulliver's Travels. There was a character in the cartoon named Glum. Glum was a pessimist. No matter what was going on, he always saw the obstacles and reasons why things weren't going to work out. Over and over, he would speak in his monotone voice, saying, "We'll never make it."

There are many Christians who are like Glum. They will often try to justify their gloomy personalities by trying to give spiritual reasons why they are never happy. They may even say things like, "Happiness depends on happenings. Spiritually mature people aren't happy- they have joy, which is different." The truth however, is that joy *is* happiness- it's a deep, abiding sense of happiness. We all experience times of sadness, but a continual gloominess of character is not spiritual maturity- it's sin.

Maybe at this point you feel like Glum. You may be one of those people who, when things don't go well, you say things like, "That's typical. Things always turn out for the worst for me. I always get the bad breaks." You may feel like "Murphy's Law" was written for you. Well, be encouraged, as you'll soon see, a life of joy is yours for the taking.

If you have been a Christian for a while, many of the truths in this book may be truths you already know in your head. But the degree to which you take these truths to heart will be the extent to which you will be able to live a life of joy. The Bible warns us, "But be doers of the word, and not hearers only, deceiving yourselves."[46] My prayer is that you will read this book prayerfully, and that God will make these truths come alive in your heart. My prayer is that this book will change your life.

In the book of Galatians, we are told, "the fruit of the Spirit is love, joy, peace, longsuffering, kindness, goodness, faithfulness, gentleness, self-control."[47] Did you notice that after love, joy is the first thing mentioned? You might think God would mention kindness, goodness and faithfulness before He mentions joy, but He doesn't. Joy is at the top of the list, right after love. Joy is the "fruit of the Spirit" and is a very important part of God's plan for us. Every one of us can walk in joy as we learn to walk in His Spirit.

The Joy of the Lord is Your Strength

A lot of Christians have what we like to call "life verses." They are verses in the Bible that God has spoken to us powerfully through and they have impacted our lives. I feel a little ashamed to admit this, but my life verse is a verse that for many years, I didn't really understand. It is found in the book of Nehemiah- "the joy of the Lord is your strength."[48] I read this verse as a brand new Christian. It seemed to almost jump off the page at me. I thought, "The joy of the Lord is my strength? What does that mean?" The verse kept coming to mind. Over and over through the years, that passage of Scripture has fascinated me. I have thought about it hundreds of times- pondering on it, reflecting, wondering, studying and

---

[46] James 1:22
[47] Galatians 5:22-23
[48] Nehemiah 8:10

praying about it. At first, I had a hard time believing it. The joy of the Lord is our strength?

Yes, there is an incredible amount of strength to be found in the joy that comes from God. The joy of the Lord can be your strength to get up every morning. It can give you strength to want to spend time with God in prayer. It will give you a desire to know God more fully. It will help you to endure difficulties in life that others would not be able to deal with. The joy of the Lord can be the wind in your sails that gets you through the toughest storms imaginable. It will help you to accomplish things you never would have dreamed were possible. It will help you remain faithful when you are being tempted, to be victorious when it would be easy to fail, to endure to the end, and to finish strong- very strong.

God's desire is that your life would be filled with that joy. His desire is that "you rejoice with joy inexpressible."[49] Doesn't that sound great- "joy inexpressible"? It's a joy so great that there are no words that can adequately describe it. That's what He wants for us in this life. As we explore more about joy in this book, we will see the wonderful benefits and the strength that come from the joy we can only get from God.

Supernatural Joy

It's important that we realize that the joy God has for us is different from the joy that comes from the things of this world. Jesus tells us that He is the vine, and we as His followers, are the branches, and that we are to "abide" in Him. He went on to say, "These things I have spoken to you, that My joy may remain in you, and that your joy may be full."[50] The joy He wants us to experience is His joy. It's supernatural. It comes from God Himself. He is the source and the power of the joy. Of course, when we receive His joy, it becomes ours. And it's not like the joy you get when someone says something

---

[49] 1 Peter 1:8
[50] John 15:11

nice to you or you get something you want. It's far richer and deeper. It's fulfilling, enriching and life sustaining.

As a result of His joy remaining in us, He wants our joy to be full. He doesn't just want us to experience a little bit of joy, or even a medium amount of joy. He wants us to have fullness of joy, ultimate joy, super joy, awesome joy. If we only abide in Him a little, we will only experience a little of His joy. The more we "abide" in Him, the more joy we will have in our lives. The key to all of this is not to get more *from* God. The key is to get more *of* God. As we learn to live a life of abiding in Christ, we experience Him abiding in us and we will have fullness of joy.

> **The more we "abide" in Him, the more joy we will have in our lives. The key to all of this is not to get more from God. The key is to get more of God.**

Jesus says, "Come to me."[51] He invites and commands all of us to come to Him, that we might have eternal life. He forgives our sins and gives us eternal life as a free gift when we turn to God and receive Jesus as our Lord and Savior. But once we come to Jesus, He says, "Abide in Me."[52] The choice to abide in Him is ours to make. We can choose to abide in Him and live in joy. So how do we abide in Jesus?

On Three

Abiding in Christ is not something that comes naturally to us. It's something we need to learn how to do. In order for me to demonstrate this point, try this. On the count of three, abide in Christ. Ready? One, two, three, go! ... How'd you do? Did it work? Were you abiding in Christ? In a way, it could be compared to learning to drive a car. It takes some time and practice, but once we learn how to do it, it's not difficult and it sure makes our travels better. Of course, if learning how to abide in Christ was as easy as learning to drive a car, the Bible

---

[51] Matthew 11:28
[52] John 15:4

would probably be a lot smaller book. We need to be willing to learn and to work at it. Whether or not we abide in Christ and have fullness of joy is up to us.

The great news is that it's not rocket science. You don't need to be smart in order to figure out how to abide in Christ. You and I can do it too. I have a friend who is a nuclear physicist who is wonderful at abiding in Christ, and yet it's so simple, a child can do it.

There are quite a few things that will bring us joy as we seek to abide in Christ. As we will see in the next chapter, there is one place where the ultimate joy will be found.

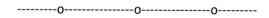

Heavenly Father, Thank You for being the God who wants to fill my life with joy. I want to experience "joy inexpressible." I want my life to be filled with Your joy. I pray that by the time I finish reading this book, and even today, my life will be changed. Help me to take the truths in this book to heart. Help me to know that the things of this world won't give me the kind of joy that only You can give me. Help me to be open to Your leading, not only as I read this book, but all day, every day. In Jesus' name I pray, Amen.

2

The Place of Joy

**"In Your presence is fullness of joy;
at Your right hand are pleasures forevermore."**

- Psalm 16:11

Fullness of Joy

People say, "There's nothing like the feeling of being in love." "There's nothing like the thrill of being on a roller coaster." "There's nothing like the feeling you get when you've saved someone's life." "There's nothing like the feeling you get when you lead someone to Christ or help change someone's life." It may be hard to imagine anything better than the wonderful feelings of joy that we may have experienced in this life. But for those of us who are trusting in Jesus, there is going to come a time when we will experience something better- far better.

There may have been times in your life when you felt an amazing sense of God's presence- when you felt such love, peace and joy, that you didn't know if you could contain it. It is a wonderful experience to be in the presence of God. But even the greatest moments of joy and bliss of God's presence you may (or may not) have experienced in this life are nothing compared to what we will experience when we get to Heaven and we see Him. Scripture tells us that in this life, "we know in part,"[1] but when we are in Heaven, we will see Him "face to face."[2] You may be thinking, "It's nice that Heaven will be

---

[1] 1 Corinthians 13:12
[2] 1 Corinthians 13:12

great, but what about my life today and tomorrow?" That's a good question, but as we will soon see, what Heaven is like can make a tremendous difference in our life today and tomorrow. For now, let's explore what Heaven will be like.

God is love.[3] He is absolute goodness.[4] He created every single thing of beauty that has ever been created. He created light, the rainbow, sunrises and sunsets, water, flowers, cool breezes, the cuteness of babies and puppies, food, colors, warmth, touch, the taste of delicious food, music, laughter, life, healing, joy, peace, hope and love- He is the source of it all. He is the source of everything good. Being in Heaven with God, you will experience more love than you have ever known, and experience more joy, more peace, more comfort, more contentment and more bliss than you have ever imagined. You will know His love in a way that you have never known it before. Being in His presence in Heaven is going to be more awesome than any of us can even imagine. As the Apostle Paul wrote, "Eye has not seen, nor ear heard, nor have entered into the heart of man the things which God has prepared for those who love Him."[5] Think of the best thing you can possibly imagine. Heaven will be better. You could spend days on end, trying to imagine better and better things- great and beautiful things, awesome things- Heaven will be better. We cannot even imagine how wonderful Heaven will be. It has not even "entered into the heart of man the things which God has prepared" for us.

A Room with a View

And you know what? Heaven is a real place. Many people, even some Christians, think Heaven is either a state of mind, or an emotional state of bliss. It's not. Heaven is a place, just like New Jersey and London are places, except that New Jersey and London won't last forever. Heaven will.

---

[3] John 4:8
[4] Psalm 136:1
[5] 1 Corinthians 2:9

Right before Jesus left the earth, He said to His followers, "In My Father's house are many mansions; if it were not so, I would have told you. I go to prepare a place for you. And if I go and prepare a place for you, I will come again and receive you to Myself; that where I am, there you may be also."[6] He didn't say, "I go to prepare a state of mind." He said, "I go to prepare a place." Heaven is a place.

Notice also that Jesus didn't just say, "I go to prepare a place." He said, "I go to prepare a place for you." God knows every single thing there is to know about you and He's preparing (or has already finished preparing) a place especially for you. Jesus didn't say, "I go to prepare a place and I hope you are ok with it." It's not like when you go into someone's house and see their wall colors and say, "Wow. I would never want to live in a house with purple walls." No. The place Jesus is preparing is designed just for you. As He said, in His Father's house are many "mansions." That word could also be translated as "dwelling places." Does that mean we each get our own mansion or bedroom in Heaven? The Bible doesn't say, but we know that God has designed these many dwelling places with each of us in mind.

The book of Hebrews tells us that Abraham "waited for the city which has foundations, whose builder and maker is God."[7] During his life, Abraham was not just looking forward to finding a wonderful state of mind; he was waiting and looking forward to going to a city that God has designed and built. Hebrews Chapter 11 tells us that others who were believers in God before us, were also desiring a Heavenly country and not an earthly one.[8] What God has prepared for us is not just "heaven on earth," it's a real place where we get to go. It could be said that Heaven is more "real" than the earth. Everything you see on earth is temporary. Heaven is eternal.

---

[6] John 14:2-3
[7] Hebrews 11:10
[8] Hebrews 11:14-16

A Place Like No Other

We don't know exactly what eternity in Heaven will be like, but the Bible gives some descriptions that give us an idea. The Bible says, "And God will wipe away every tear from their eyes; there shall be no more death, nor sorrow, nor crying. There shall be no more pain, for the former things have passed away."[9] There are many, many wonderful things about Heaven. For one thing, Heaven is a place of absolute comfort. We may experience a lot of emotional pain in this life. Sometimes we are healed from the pain we suffer. Sometimes we may be hurt deeply and not experience a complete healing from the wounds- but we will be completely healed in Heaven. We may have regrets about things we've done (or not done) in this life. In Heaven, we will be comforted.[10]

Will there be crying in Heaven? If there is, it will only be for a moment. We'll leave our tears at the door. Every tear that we cry for anything will be wiped away by God Himself.[11] An angel won't wipe away our tears- God will. We won't walk through a machine with an automatic tear wiper. And God won't just wipe away some of our tears- He will wipe away every tear. What could we be sad about? Maybe we'll be grieving from things we had suffered on the earth. He will wipe away every tear. Maybe we will be sorry that we didn't live a life that was worthy of Him. Maybe we'll be grieving about people who didn't make it to Heaven. It doesn't matter what the source of our sorrow may be- He will wipe away every tear. He is the "God of all comfort."[12] There will be no sorrow.[13] Isn't that awesome? You will have no sadness about

---

[9] Revelation 21:4
[10] Luke 16:25
[11] Revelation 7:17
[12] 2 Corinthians 1:3
[13] Revelation 21:4

anything, ever again. In Heaven, God Himself will comfort you with His absolutely perfect comfort.

There will be no pain in Heaven.[14] I can't wait. I sometimes joke when people ask me if I have any allergies. I say, "Yes, I'm allergic to pain." I am looking forward to being in that place where there is absolutely no pain.

Some of us suffer in this life from chronic illnesses. In Heaven, we will be healed.[15] There will be no sickness.[16] Isn't that awesome? There will be no heart disease, no cancer, no strokes, no diabetes, no arthritis, no Alzheimer's disease or dementia, no colds or flu, no pneumonia or coughs, no sore backs or achy joints, no cuts or bruises, no sprained ankles, no sores, no ear aches, no tooth aches, no trips or falls, no hospitals or doctors treating patients, and no car accidents.

There will be no death.[17] That means we will not be getting old or decaying. We won't get wrinkles or age spots. Nobody will have dentures or crutches or wheelchairs or glasses. That is one of the wonderful things about Heaven-our bodies will never wear out. We will live forever!

It all sounds so good. It's hard to imagine being free from all pain, sickness, sorrow, suffering and death. Does it sound too good to be true? It's no wonder that right after telling us about it, God reassures us by inserting a verse saying, "Write, for these words are true and faithful."[18]

All around us, we see things getting older and falling apart. Of course, it's not just our bodies that get old. Beautiful new cars get old, break down, rust and eventually end up in junk yards. Clothes wear out and end up in the trash. Houses wear out. Everything around us is getting older. Astronomers tell us that the entire universe is getting older and wearing out. It's suffering a slow death from heat loss. It's falling

---

[14] Revelation 21:4
[15] Revelation 22:2
[16] Isaiah 33:24
[17] Revelation 21:4
[18] Revelation 21:5

apart. Even the stars in the sky won't last forever- they're getting older. In fact, "the heavens" (the sky) and the earth will be destroyed by fire and God will make a new heaven (sky[19]) and earth.[20] The new earth and sky will never wear out. They will last forever.

The Ultimate Security

Most of us have material things we value. Whether they are houses, money, cars, clothes or other material possessions, they are always at risk. We could lose them either by fire, theft or simply by them wearing out, rusting, or being eaten by moths or termites. It won't be that way in Heaven. There is no rust in Heaven. Moths won't eat anyone's clothes.[21] Termites won't eat anyone's houses. People say, "Nothing lasts forever." Well, in Heaven, everything will last forever. You'll never have to worry about anyone stealing anything from you.[22] In fact, you won't worry about anything at all. There will be no burglaries, robberies or padlocks. There won't be any identity theft, and you won't ever lose anything. In Heaven, our treasures will be absolutely safe.

Heavenly Treasure, Treasurely Heaven

Not only will our treasures be safe in Heaven, but Heaven itself will be a treasure. It's beautiful beyond our wildest dreams. The descriptions of Heaven given in the Bible are so amazing, they are difficult to even imagine. When we look at a beautiful sunrise or sunset, or see the majesty of a clear, starry night, a beautiful mountain range or a powerful waterfall, we are in awe. The Bible tells us that "the heavens

---

[19] The same Greek word is used in the Bible for Heaven and for the sky (the "heavens") although they are two different things. The context of the verses makes clear which meaning is intended.
[20] 2 Peter 3:7-13
[21] Matthew 6:20
[22] Matthew 6:20

declare the glory of God."[23] The universe is an incredibly awesome place. I took an astronomy class in college. It was there I began to grasp just how vast our universe is. Astronomers think there are between 200-400 billion stars in our Milky Way Galaxy and there are hundreds of billions of galaxies. It's estimated that the universe is more than 100 billion light years across. (One light year is about 5.8 trillion miles.) It's easy to get lost trying to comprehend just how big and magnificent the universe is. It's mind boggling. Looking at the images taken from the Hubble telescope is quite an experience. (You can see amazing images at: www.hubblesite.org) God's creation is amazing beyond description, and yet it can't compare to what Heaven will be like.

The Apostle John was given a revelation of Heaven. He said, "behold, a throne set in heaven, and One sat on the throne. And He who sat there was like a jasper and a sardius stone in appearance; and there was a rainbow around the throne, in appearance like an emerald."[24] Heaven is an incredibly beautiful place. God Himself is so beautiful and majestic that we can only begin to imagine what He looks like. John describes God as looking like a jasper stone and a sardius stone, and being surrounded by a rainbow that looks like an emerald. So, according to John's description, God's shining brilliance is like precious gem stones and the colors that shine forth from Him are reds and greens. Lightning and thunder come from the throne of God, along with voices. There are seven lamps of fire in front of the throne which are the seven Spirits of God.[25] In front of the throne, there is "a sea of glass, like crystal."[26] The beauty of Heaven must be incredible. The beautiful colors and emerald rainbow, with lightning and lamps of fire all reflecting off the crystal sea- it's

---

[23] Psalm 19:1
[24] Revelation 4:3
[25] Revelation 4:5
[26] Revelation 4:6

definitely hard to imagine, but one thing we can be sure of- its beauty is far beyond anything we have ever seen or can even picture in our minds.

Heaven will be a place where all of us will be rich beyond our wildest dreams, not with money, but with treasures that are far greater than anything we have ever known- we will inherit Heaven![27] Jesus said "Then the King will say to those on His right hand, 'Come, you blessed of My Father, inherit the kingdom prepared for you from the foundation of the world.'"[28] Jesus paid the ultimate price so we can receive the ultimate prize. There will be no poverty in Heaven, nobody asking for handouts and nobody going hungry. Every one of us will have absolutely everything we need and everything we will want. Heaven is a place of absolute satisfaction and abundance. None of us will be saying, "Oh, if only I had _____." Heaven will be complete for every one of us. We will be in absolute joy, absolute peace and absolute splendor.

> **Jesus paid the ultimate price so we can receive the ultimate prize.**

John used human words to describe what Heaven looks like, but we know the wording can't even come close to describing just how truly awesome God and Heaven are. It's like trying to describe a beautiful sunset to a person who is blind, or the beautiful melody of a song bird to a person who is deaf. We know it's going to be great, but we really have no idea of how great.

We have never seen the throne of God, or anything like it, so it is impossible for us to imagine, but we know from John's description that it is a marvelous sight. Of course, it will be the beauty and splendor of God Himself that really makes Heaven beautiful. The splendor and majesty of God is vastly more amazing than anything anyone can possibly imagine.

---

[27] Matthew 25:34
[28] Matthew 25:34

A City from Heaven

Part of our Heavenly experience will be the New Jerusalem. The Bible describes the New Jerusalem as an enormous city that is about 1400 miles wide, 1400 miles long and 1400 miles high.[29] The New Jerusalem will come down out of Heaven and will be magnificent. It will be illuminated by the glory of God Himself. In the book of Revelation, the Apostle John describes how he was shown the New Jerusalem by an angel, "And he carried me away in the Spirit to a great and high mountain, and showed me the great city, the holy Jerusalem, descending out of heaven from God, having the glory of God. Her light was like a most precious stone, like a jasper stone, clear as crystal. Also, she had a great and high wall with twelve gates, and twelve angels at the gates... The construction of its wall was of jasper; and the city was pure gold, like clear glass. The foundations of the wall of the city were adorned with all kinds of precious stones,"[30] including jasper, sapphire, chalcedony, emerald, sardonyx, sardius, chrysolite, beryl, topaz, chrysoprase, jacinth, and amethyst.[31] "The twelve gates were twelve pearls: each individual gate was of one pearl. And the street of the city was pure gold, like transparent glass. But I saw no temple in it, for the Lord God Almighty and the Lamb are its temple. The city had no need of the sun or of the moon to shine in it, for the glory of God illuminated it. The Lamb is its light."[32]

The New Jerusalem will be an absolutely spectacular place. The glory of God will be shining and lighting the entire city. Surrounding the city, there will be a 200 foot high wall made of Jasper stone with beautiful gemstones as its foundation. The radiance of God's glory will shine through the 200 foot high gemstone wall. The gates to the city will be

---

[29] Revelation 21:16
[30] Revelation 21:10-12, 18-19
[31] Revelation 21:19-20
[32] Revelation 21:21-23

giant pearls. The city and its streets will be made of pure gold. Gold is one of the most treasured things on earth. In the New Jerusalem, it will be what the walls of the buildings and the pavement on the streets are made of. Truly, the glory of Heaven and the New Jerusalem are impossible to fully comprehend.

Things We Won't Have in Heaven

Heaven will be spectacular beyond our wildest dreams. And one of the many things we'll love about Heaven, is what's not there. As we've looked at, there will be no tears, death, sorrow, crying, pain, guilt, regrets, sickness, poverty, rust, moths, termites,[33] or theft.[34] Two of the things I am most looking forward to not being in Heaven are temptation and sin. As we are told in the book of Revelation- "But there shall by no means enter it anything that defiles, or causes an abomination or a lie."[35] When we get to Heaven, our true Home, we will never struggle again with the temptation to sin.

Jesus told us to pray, "Your will be done on earth as it is in Heaven."[36] In Heaven, God's will is done. It is perfect there. There will be no crimes committed in Heaven and no sin of any kind. It will be perfect. Paul wrote about the struggle we have in our earthly bodies, saying, "For I delight in the law of God according to the inward man. But I see another law in my members, warring against the law of my mind, and bringing me into captivity to the law of sin which is in my members. O wretched man that I am! Who will deliver me from this body of death?"[37] When we are delivered from this "body of death" (our earthly body) we "will be delivered from the bondage of corruption into the glorious liberty of the children of God."[38]

---

[33] At least they won't be destroying things- see Matthew 6:20
[34] Matthew 6:20
[35] Revelation 21:27
[36] Matthew 6:10; Luke 11:2
[37] Romans 7:22-24
[38] Romans 8:21

We will be completely free from sin. How wonderful that will be. As Paul says, "even we ourselves groan within ourselves, eagerly waiting for the adoption, the redemption of our body."[39] When we get our new bodies, we will experience a liberty and a freedom that we have never known. It will be amazing!

Reunited

Another great thing about Heaven is that we will never again have any feelings of loneliness. We will be with our Wonderful Lord, Savior and God- in person, face to face. It will be awesome. We will also be with all of those people who lived throughout the ages who have put their trust in Christ. From Noah, to Abraham, Sarah, Isaac, Jacob, Joseph, Moses, David, Samuel, Gideon, Samson, John, Mary, Peter, James, and Paul (the list goes on and on). Of course, it will be wonderful to see our own believing friends as well as our family members who have gone on before us- not only those who we have known, but distant relatives: great, great grandparents and great uncles and aunts who we've never met- believers who will have wonderful stories to tell. They will all be there and we will get to spend eternity with them. There may be things that bother us about some Christians we know here on earth. In Heaven, there won't be anything about them that bothers us, or anything about us that bothers them. We will be made perfect- mature and complete. None of us will have any irritating qualities. We will live in absolute harmony with one another. We will be one.

You might have lost a loved one- a child or a believing spouse or family member, and you may carry the scars in your heart of that incredible loss. When we are in Heaven, you will see them again. When King David's son died, he said, "I shall go to him," and just as he knew that he would see his son again, you can know that you will see your child or believing

---

[39] Romans 8:23

loved ones again. It's just a matter of time, and as we will see, the time will be short.

Will We Recognize Each Other In Heaven?

Some people worry that in Heaven we might look very different than we look now, or there will be some other reason why we won't recognize each other. I like what the late Pastor Chuck Smith said when asked whether we will recognize each other in Heaven. He said, "Well, I don't think we'll be any stupider there than we are here." In the book of Matthew, we are told, "Jesus took Peter, James, and John his brother, led them up on a high mountain by themselves; and He was transfigured before them. His face shone like the sun, and His clothes became as white as the light. And behold, Moses and Elijah appeared to them, talking with Him. Then Peter answered and said to Jesus, 'Lord, it is good for us to be here; if You wish, let us make here three tabernacles: one for You, one for Moses, and one for Elijah.'"[40] It's highly unlikely that Moses and Elijah had name tags on. Peter, James and John just knew who they were. The Apostle Paul says "For now we see in a mirror dimly, but then face to face; now I know in part, but then I will know fully just as I also have been fully known."[41] We will know each other in Heaven, and we will enjoy our time with each other more than we ever did on this earth. Everything in Heaven will be better than it is on this earth.

The Cardboard Sunset

We know that "Eye has not seen, nor ear heard, nor have entered into the heart of man the things which God has prepared for those who love Him."[42] We can't even imagine how good and beautiful and glorious Heaven will be. Paul said

---

[40] Matthew 17:1-4
[41] 1 Corinthians 13:12 (NASB)
[42] 1 Corinthians 2:9

"we see in a mirror, dimly."[43] In Paul's day, they hadn't perfected making mirrors. They used polished metal and it wouldn't give a perfect reflection. It was distorted. And Paul said we see "dimly" or "darkly." His point is that we can't really see some things very well. It might be compared to someone making a cardboard model of a beautiful sunset for someone who has never seen a sunset. A cardboard sunset just can't compare to a real sunset. In the same way, we really have no idea of just how wonderful Heaven will be.

What Are We Going To Do There?

Around and in front of the throne of God are assembled Heavenly beings- "And they do not rest day or night, saying: "Holy, holy, holy, Lord God Almighty, Who was and is and is to come!"[44]

> A cardboard sunset just can't compare to a real sunset. In the same way, we really have no idea of just how wonderful Heaven will be.

So Heaven is a place of continual worship. I like to think of it like this- God's glory is so amazing, it is a little like standing in front of a giant diamond or emerald. One glance at the glory, beauty and majesty of God results in the four living creatures bowing down in worship, awed by the glory of God. They bow down, saying, "Holy, holy, holy, Lord God Almighty, Who was and is and is to come!" Then they look back up and see another glimpse of the glory, splendor and majesty of God, and again bow down in worship, saying "Holy, holy, holy, Lord God Almighty, Who was and is and is to come!" Then they look up again at God and marvel, and they bow down and worship some more. As the verse says, "they do not rest day or night."[45] It's not that they aren't allowed to rest- they don't need or want to rest. God is so awesome and glorious that these four living creatures could do this for eternity and every

---

[43] 1 Corinthians 13:12
[44] Revelation 4:8
[45] Revelation 4:8

time they look at God, they would again be amazed and in awe. They will give glory and honor and thanks to God forever. That is how awesome our God is.

There are 24 "elders," clothed in white robes, with gold crowns, on thrones around the throne of God. They will throw their crowns down before the throne of God, and like the four living creatures, they too will worship God. They say, "You are worthy, O Lord, to receive glory and honor and power; for You created all things, and by Your will they exist and were created."[46]

But it isn't just the living creatures and the 24 elders in Heaven worshipping God- there are also angels, lots of them, "Then I looked, and I heard the voice of many angels around the throne, the living creatures, and the elders; and the number of them was ten thousand times ten thousand, and thousands of thousands, saying with a loud voice: 'Worthy is the Lamb who was slain to receive power and riches and wisdom, and strength and honor and glory and blessing!'"[47] Ten thousand times ten thousand, and thousands of thousands of angels- that's more than 100 million angels!

The largest stadium in the world is in the Czech Republic. It holds 220,000 people. That's a huge stadium that holds a lot of people, but it's nothing compared to more than 100 million angels gathered around the throne of God in Heaven. They will worship Jesus loudly, saying, "Worthy is the Lamb who was slain to receive power and riches and wisdom, and strength and honor and glory and blessing!"[48] And it won't just be the angels that are worshipping God- "And every creature which is in heaven and on the earth and under the earth and such as are in the sea, and all that are in them, I heard saying: 'Blessing and honor and glory and power be to Him who sits on the throne, and to the Lamb, forever and

---

[46] Revelation 4:11
[47] Revelation 5:11-12
[48] Revelation 5:11-12

ever!'"49 It's impossible to imagine just how glorious and awesome that will be.

The Mood in Heaven

What do you think the mood in Heaven will be like? Do you picture God and the angels as being very serious all the time? If so, you are mistaken. Jesus tells us, "there is joy in the presence of the angels of God over one sinner who repents."50 So if the angels have joy over one sinner turning to God, and (somewhere on earth) people are turning to God every second of every day, it doesn't paint a very somber picture of the angels in Heaven. They must be quite a happy bunch.

How about God? Do you picture Him as being serious all the time or having no emotion? The prophet Zephaniah speaks of God's reaction to His people and says, "He will rejoice over you with gladness... He will rejoice over you with singing."51 Some people might think this must be figurative language and that God wouldn't really sing for joy over His people- that it would be below His dignity. They might question whether Almighty God would engage in singing of any kind. I believe God meant what He said. He will sing for joy over us. If you think about it, it's enough to bring tears to one's eyes- that Almighty God would sing for joy over us. Isaiah says, "the LORD delights in you... and as the bridegroom rejoices over the bride, so shall your God rejoice over you."52 "As a bridegroom delights and rejoices over the bride"? That's quite a bit of delight and rejoicing. In describing the Kingdom of Heaven, Jesus said God is like an earthly father who, when his son returns to him, says, "Bring out the best robe and put it on him, and put a ring on his hand and sandals on his feet. And bring the fatted calf here and kill

---

49 Revelation 5:13
50 Luke 15:10
51 Zephaniah 3:17
52 Isaiah 62:4, 5

it, and let us eat and be merry; for this my son was dead and is alive again; he was lost and is found."[53] He says, "we should make merry and be glad."[54]

We've got to get over the terrible notion that God is like a giant grumpy old man sitting in Heaven, or that He is some kind of massive energy field with no feelings. He is our Heavenly Father. We were created in His image.[55] The Bible says God "takes pleasure in His people."[56] He experiences pleasure. In God's presence is fullness of joy.[57] That doesn't mean everyone around God is in fullness of joy, but God is emotionless. It won't just be people and angels that are joyful in Heaven. No, God Himself will be full of joy! Our God is the God of joy- the Creator and source of true joy. Jesus said the faithful servant would be rewarded and would be told, "Enter into the joy of your lord."[58] When we get to Heaven, we will enter into the joy of our Lord- we will enter *His* joy- the joy of God. In fact, when we get to Heaven, there will be a giant wedding feast- the "marriage supper of the Lamb."[59] Many Bible teachers believe this party will actually last for seven years![60] Is Heaven a very holy place- a very awesome place? Yes, but Heaven is also a very happy place. King Solomon tells us, "whoever trusts in the LORD, happy is he."[61] Well, in Heaven, "happy" will be taken to a whole new level. It's no wonder we'll need new bodies in Heaven. These bodies we have now just wouldn't be able to contain the joy we will have, being in God's presence!

---

[53] Luke 15:22-24
[54] Luke 15:32
[55] Genesis 1:26-27
[56] Psalm 149:4
[57] Psalm 16:11
[58] Matthew 25:21
[59] Revelation 19:9
[60] Corresponding to the 69th "week" of Daniel Chapter 9
[61] Proverbs 16:20

A verse in one of the most wonderful and popular Hymns of all time, Amazing Grace, says, "When we've been there ten thousand years, bright shining as the sun, we've no less days to sing God's praise, than when we first begun." Some people seem to think Heaven will be more like a funeral than a feast. They think Heaven sounds like a boring place. They think there will be nothing to do but sit around on clouds all day, strumming harps. They have no idea what God and Heaven are like. I even heard a "Christian" speaker make fun of that verse in Amazing Grace. He said, "'When we've been there ten thousand years, we've no less days to sing God's praise, than when we first begun.'? I don't know about you, but standing in church, singing for ten thousand years doesn't sound like fun to me." He then proceeded to explain how his version of Heaven involved all sorts of sporting activities like kayaking and snow skiing. I believe that like those who think Heaven sounds like a boring place, he really doesn't have a clue as to how awesome God is and how wonderful Heaven will be. Will we be enjoying every single moment in Heaven far more than we ever enjoyed any moment on earth? Absolutely; even in this life, God gives us "all things to enjoy,"[62] and Heaven will be "far better,"[63] but we won't need to do any kayaking in Heaven in order for our joy to be full. It will make any sport or thrill we had on this earth seem like a cough!

> **The thrill of being in Heaven will make any sport or thrill we had on this earth seem like a cough!**

God Will Serve Us

Jesus suffered and died on the cross for your sins. He paid the ultimate price so that you and I could be in Heaven with Him. Heaven is going to be awesome, and it's going to last forever. You might think that God has already done too much for us. We could never deserve what He is giving us for

---

[62] 1 Timothy 6:17
[63] Philippians 1:23

free- forgiveness, a personal relationship with Him, and eternity in Heaven to top it off! But He's not done giving yet.

In Luke Chapter 12, Jesus tells us about what it will be like for those who are waiting for His return. He said, "Blessed are those servants whom the master, when he comes, will find watching. Assuredly, I say to you that he will gird himself and have them sit down to eat, and will come and serve them."[64] Jesus told us that in Heaven, He will actually serve us. We, as followers of Jesus, are called the "bride" of Christ.[65] When we are in Heaven, we will attend the marriage supper of the Lamb.[66] In a first century Jewish wedding, the "marriage supper," or "wedding feast," took place after the bride and groom were united together. When we get to Heaven, we will sit down and eat with the Lord, the Creator of the universe, and He will serve us. It's hard to imagine. We are so unworthy. Our God is the God who loves to bless us- and He will never stop blessing us. That's the heart of our God.

Will We Have to Work in Heaven?

The Bible also tells us that in Heaven we will serve God.[67] You might think, "I thought Heaven was going to be like a vacation. I thought I wouldn't have to do any work. I was looking forward to getting some rest." The reality is that doing work in Heaven is nothing like doing work on earth. When Adam and Eve disobeyed God in the Garden of Eden, it resulted in mankind being subjected to "the curse."[68] Part of the curse has been that work involves a lot of effort. The word used in the Bible is "toil."[69] The word could also be translated as "pain, labor, hardship, or sorrow." We won't have pain,

---

[64] Luke 12:37
[65] Revelation 19:7-9; Ephesians 5:25-27; 2 Corinthians 11:2
[66] Revelation 19:9
[67] Revelation 22:3
[68] Genesis 3
[69] NKJV

suffering, or sorrow in Heaven, so we know that working in Heaven will be radically different than working on earth. You can rest assured that any work you do in Heaven will be far more pleasurable than the best vacation you've ever had.

Sometimes you talk to someone who says they have the perfect job. It's great that they love their job, but in reality, they don't really have a perfect job. Nobody on earth does. In Heaven we will all say, "I love my job! It's perfect. I wouldn't trade it for the world." And we will mean it. In the book of Ephesians, we are told that we are God's "workmanship."[70] That word in Greek is "poiema," the same word from which we get the English word "poem." We are His craftsmanship. And we are told that we were "created in Christ Jesus for good works, which God prepared beforehand that we should walk in them."[71] The work we will do in Heaven is work we were designed to do. It will be an absolutely perfect fit and will be such a joy to do; we will praise God continually for blessing us by allowing us to do it. It will be nothing like the burdensome "toil" we have to do now on the earth. In fact, we will not even have the same kind of bodies we have now.[72] God will give us a new and improved version of our bodies, and we will never get one bit tired from serving our Wonderful God. Serving Him will be absolute, pure joy. There will be no curse and no toil. It will be absolute pleasure.

What Do You Need?

A lot of our time on this earth is spent taking care of our basic needs. God provides for us, just as He does for the grass in the field, but we also have to work for it. We need food, clothing and shelter. (For us Americans, we generally think the list is a lot longer than that.) God has prepared places for us to live in Heaven;[73] we won't ever be concerned about

---

[70] Ephesians 2:10
[71] Ephesians 2:10
[72] 1 Corinthians 15:50-53
[73] John 14:2

where our next meal is coming from. "They shall neither hunger anymore nor thirst anymore."[74] We won't be concerned about how the rent or mortgage will be paid, where we are going to live, or what we are going to eat or wear. As the Apostle John tells us, in Heaven there is "a pure river of water of life, clear as crystal, proceeding from the throne of God and of the Lamb. In the middle of its street, and on either side of the river, was the tree of life, which bore twelve fruits, each tree yielding its fruit every month."[75] Heaven is a place of abundance and complete provision. Every one of our needs will continually be met.

In Heaven, there will be nothing, absolutely nothing to worry about. We will be completely safe at all times. We will be perfectly comfortable at all times as well. We will never get hot[76] or cold in Heaven. If we will be able to feel temperature in Heaven, you can rest assured the thermostat will always be set to "perfect."

Time for a Nap

We all get tired. It may be the tiredness that comes from hard work or at the end of a long day, or from exercise. It could be from health issues, we could be tired of suffering, or it may be in a season of life when we just feel tired. Whatever the cause, we all know what it's like to be tired. One of the wonderful things about Heaven is that it is described as a place of rest.[77] There will be no struggling, or stress, or exhaustion. What an awesome thing it will be for us to enter that place of complete and total rest.

The Best Thing of All

The glory and beauty of Heaven are impossible to fully imagine. The absolute bliss we will experience as we enter

---

[74] Revelation 7:16
[75] Revelation 22:1-2
[76] Revelation 7:16
[77] Hebrews 4:1; Revelation 14:13

that place of eternal joy is beyond our ability to comprehend now. There is one thing, however, that will be better than everything else in Heaven- the presence of God. As the psalmist wrote, "In Your presence is fullness of joy; At Your right hand are pleasures forevermore."[78] Being in God's presence will be so amazingly awesome, it will make everything else pale in comparison. The best thing about Heaven is that God is there. He is the source of everything good, and as the Apostle John wrote in the book of Revelation, "And I heard a loud voice from heaven saying, 'Behold, the tabernacle of God is with men, and He will dwell with them, and they shall be His people. God Himself will be with them and be their God.'"[79] We can barely begin to grasp the magnitude of that statement, "God Himself will be with them and be their God."

The God who created the universe will be with us for all of eternity as our Creator, our God, our Savior, and our Friend. Being in His presence will make anything we have ever suffered in this life seem like nothing. As the Apostle Paul said, "the sufferings of this present time are not worthy to be compared with the glory which shall be revealed in us."[80] Like a woman who gives birth and soon after forgets the pain she endured in labor, we will soon be so full of joy in His presence, that anything we suffer in this life will seem like less than nothing. We will be in fullness of joy forever.

Jesus is called, "'Immanuel,' which is translated, 'God with us.'"[81] As people who have decided to follow Jesus, we have Him with us and His Holy Spirit in us, but in Heaven, we will be face to face with Him, and it will be absolute bliss forever.

In this world, our joys are often mixed with sorrow. We face disappointment, loss, grief, guilt, trials and worry. In

---

[78] Psalm 16:11
[79] Revelation 21:3
[80] Romans 8:18
[81] Matthew 1:23

Heaven, our joy will be 100% full. There will be no sin, no pain, sorrow, sickness, loss, disappointment, guilt, grief, regrets, fear, anger, toil, loneliness, suffering, sadness, death or despair. Heaven is a place of absolute joy, total comfort, perfect healing, complete security, abundant provision, absolute rest, incredible beauty, and perfect peace. You will be in a "dwelling place," or a "mansion" that is prepared especially for you. It will be perfect- absolute pleasure and bliss. And you will be there in the presence of the amazing God who loves you with an everlasting love, not because you are good enough to go to Heaven, but because God chose you before He created the world,[82] and you will be there forever. It will never get old. To sum it up: Heaven will be a place of absolute, utter joy.[83]

You might be thinking something like, "That's going to be awesome. I can't wait. But what about today?" I'm glad you asked. In the next chapter, we are going to answer that question.

----------o----------------o----------------o---------

Heavenly Father, Thank You for being a God who loves me so much that You are going to give me eternal life in Heaven. Even though I haven't seen it yet and I can't fully imagine what it will be like, I know Heaven is going to be amazing. The beauty and majesty of Heaven are far more awesome than I can even imagine. Thank You for preparing a place in Heaven for me and for Your promises that I will never feel pain, sorrow or sickness and will live forever. Please give me a deeper understanding of what the absolute joy and pleasure of being in Heaven with You will be like. In Jesus' name I pray, Amen.

---

[82] Ephesians 1:4; Titus 3:5
[83] Psalm 16:11

3

What About Today?

"Though now you do not see Him, yet believing, you rejoice with joy inexpressible..."
- 1 Peter 1:8

What if you were going to Heaven (that place of absolute, perfect pleasure and everlasting joy) a week from today? Would you be excited? Think about how it would change your day today, tomorrow and the next day. Think about how excited you would be tonight as you prepare to go to sleep. Would the problems you have in your life really seem

> **What if you were going to Heaven a week from today? Would the problems you have in your life really seem all that bad?**

all that bad? Of course, there would be some things you would want to take care of before you leave this earth to go on that last, incredibly awesome adventure.

But would the fact that you may have health problems, really be all that big a deal? Would you really be as upset as you may be about some relationship problems you might be having, or difficulties with your spouse or boss or co-workers or neighbors, or financial problems, or problems at your job, or whatever problems? Would it matter that your life, your job or your school seem boring? If you only had a few days left on this earth before you were going to Heaven forever, wouldn't your life take on new meaning? You would look at life differently. Your priorities would change and even though your soon departure might result in you not wanting to leave some of the people and situations you have in your life now, you would have powerful reasons to be living a life of joy-Heaven would only be a few days away! Knowing that you will be experiencing indescribable joy in just a few days, would give you a great amount of joy today.

Am I Old?

At the time I am writing this book, I am 55 years old. I eat a whole-food, plant based diet and exercise fairly regularly, so I am not experiencing many of the ailments and illnesses that most Americans suffer from and I have lots of energy, but I still notice signs of aging. I've got a few gray hairs and my skin is a bit more wrinkled than it was when I was 20. I know this physical body will not live forever. As the Apostle Paul said, my "outward man is perishing,"[1] my "tent,"[2] (my body) is getting older, but I know that I have "a building from God, a house not made with hands, eternal in the heavens."[3]

It amazes me how we Americans work so hard to hang on to our youth. There were 14,600,000 cosmetic plastic surgery procedures performed in the U.S. in 2012. Over fourteen million plastic surgeries in one year! Americans now spend about $80 billion a year on anti-aging products. I read about one skin care product that costs $1,500 for a 28 day supply. I'm not saying it's wrong to want to look younger or better, but those numbers reflect just how important it is for us Americans that we look good. Isaiah the Prophet said, "All flesh is grass, and all its loveliness is like the flower of the field."[4] The beauty of a flower is amazing, but it doesn't last long. And it doesn't matter how many nips and tucks we get, our body's longevity is like grass in a field. And its beauty is like a flower. It won't last. I think of it like lettuce. Have you ever noticed how long lettuce lasts before it wilts and gets old? Not long. If you take a leaf of lettuce and put it on your

---

[1] 2 Corinthians 4:16
[2] 2 Corinthians 5:1
[3] 2 Corinthians 5:1
[4] Isaiah 40:6

kitchen counter for a few hours, you'll get a good idea of what God means when He says all flesh is like grass.[5] That's what our bodies are like- grass or lettuce.

That might sound like bad news, but it's not. We, like the Apostle Paul, can rejoice, knowing that we will get new bodies soon- better, eternal bodies. The physical bodies we have now have weaknesses, but our new bodies will be strong. They will be awesome. They will be "incorruptible,"[6] which means they won't ever wear out, get old, wrinkle, or fall apart. They will feel no pain and they will last forever! They will be glorious! They will be perfect bodies! It's no wonder why the Apostle Paul said, "For we know that if our earthly house, this tent, is destroyed, we have a building from God, a house not made with hands, eternal in the heavens."[7] He called the bodies that we have now, "tents." Would you rather live in a tent or a building, a house that God made in Heaven? Think about how much better a house on earth is than a tent. Can you imagine how much better our building in Heaven is going to be? I can't, but I know our tents can't compare to how nice our new houses will be.

We're Getting Closer

I like to think of it this way- We're not getting older, we're getting closer. Since we are trusting in Jesus Christ, we have eternal life. We are going to live forever. It's hard to think of yourself as old when you are only 50 or 100 years old and you're going to live forever. I'm excited about the fact that every day that passes is one day closer to us being in Heaven.

I want to take good care of the "tent" God has given me (to be a good steward), but one day, I'm going to leave it behind. I'm moving on, going to a place where there is no death, no pain, no sorrow, no disappointments, no guilt, no

---

[5] Although lettuce sold at some fast food restaurants have chemicals in it that could probably make it look good for weeks.

[6] 1 Corinthians 15:52

[7] 2 Corinthians 5:1

heartache, no sickness, no sin and no suffering. And if you are trusting in Jesus Christ as your Lord and Savior, you'll be going there too.

If you found out this morning that you won the Publisher's Clearinghouse Sweepstakes- $1 million in cash and $5,000 a week for life, how would tomorrow's trials seem to you? Would you be able to endure rush hour traffic without complaining, or your co-worker's difficult personality, or the possibly irritating habits of your spouse or family members?

> **If you found out this morning that you won the Publisher's Clearinghouse Sweepstakes- $1 million in cash and $5,000 a week for life, would you be able to endure tomorrow's rush hour traffic without complaining?**

If you are on the way to the bank to deposit a check for $10 million, would you say, "Oh, bummer!" when the traffic lights on the way into town that you hoped would be green, are red? Probably not. You would probably be thinking of all the things you can do with $10 million- how it can bless your life and how you can bless others.

We Win

The joy we should have about going to Heaven should make the winnings of a $10 million sweepstakes seem like sawdust. There is no comparison between what God has in store for us in Heaven, and some money (or any other treasure) here on earth. Jesus said, "Do not lay up for yourselves treasures on earth, where moth and rust destroy and where thieves break in and steal; but lay up for yourselves treasures in heaven, where neither moth nor rust destroys and where thieves do not break in and steal."[8] Our treasures in Heaven will last forever. Not only are earthly treasures going to wear out, rust, fall apart, break, or be stolen; they are only temporary. Whether we like it or not, our life on this

---

[8] Matthew 6:19-20

earth is short, like a puff of smoke rising into the air. It doesn't matter whether you are now a teenager or are 90 years old- life is very short. It may seem like you have a lot of life still in front of you, but ask anyone who is nearing the end of their days, they will tell you- life is short.

It is a tremendous blessing to visit Christians in third world countries. I've had the privilege of travelling to India three times. It changed my life. I walked into people's homes that are made of mud bricks and straw, houses with no electricity or running water. These people don't own a piece of (what we would call) furniture and have probably never even seen a toothbrush. There's no stove or microwave oven, just a few bricks stacked in a corner of a room on which the family's one pot is placed while a fire is started underneath it. Members of the family may own two items of clothing each, along with a pair of sandals for each of the parents. The entire family may live on less than two dollars a day. Most of us Westerners would see these people as having nothing.

Not only are these people materially poor, but their lives are filled with difficulties. In many cases, children may not be able to go to school because their responsibility is to get water for the family. They may spend hours every day walking to the well to get water. Even young children work in order to help provide income so the family can meet their most basic needs.

> The joy we should have about going to Heaven should make the winnings of a $10 million sweepstakes seem like sawdust.

In India, there are three hundred million Dalits (also known as "untouchables"). These are people who are born into families that are the lowest of the low in the Hindu caste system- they are considered as less than human. They are treated far worse than animals and are taught that they are living to suffer, in order to pay off their past life sins- their bad "karma." Many of them are beaten, discriminated against and persecuted, and many of the women are raped- just because they are Dalits-

"untouchables." When a Dalit becomes a Christian, they are often treated even worse.

As Having Nothing, and Yet Possessing All Things

But if you walk into a church full of Dalits, you would have no idea they live such difficult lives. In fact, the opposite is the case- you might think each of them just won a $10 million sweepstakes. There they are, sitting on a dirt floor, owning little more in this world than the clothes on their backs and a pair of sandals. They are persecuted, discriminated against, having no hope of getting out of their situations in this life, and yet they are clapping and singing to the Lord with a joy that would make a king or a rich person envious. The joy that radiates from these people is enough to make almost anyone envious. It is absolutely amazing. They are filled to overflowing with the love and joy of Christ. Where do they get it? They get it from Heaven- from their relationship with God and from their hope, their sure hope, that when they leave this earth, they will be going to a city whose builder and maker is God. They know that this life is short and that Heaven will last forever.

There are many Christians around the world that live in what most of us Westerners would call, terrible situations. They are persecuted, discriminated against, and are living in poverty; but when you meet them, you can't help but wonder, "What do they have that I don't? Why are they so happy?" You could say that it all comes down to one word- focus.

In the book of Hebrews, we are told that, "faith is the substance of things hoped for, the evidence of things not seen."[9] We see that faith is the "substance," or the "assurance" of things hoped for. Our faith is inextricably linked to our future hope. In fact, the writer of Hebrews commends the Hebrew believers, saying they "joyfully accepted" the plundering of their goods, knowing that they have a better

---

[9] Hebrews 11:1

and an enduring possession for themselves in Heaven.[10] What was their secret? How could they possibly "joyfully accept" having everything they owned stolen from them? They did it by looking to the future.

The Focus of Faith

These believers were not living their lives focusing on the things of this world. No, they desired "a better country, that is, a heavenly one."[11] Their focus was on eternal things. Like Abraham, they "waited for the city which has foundations, whose builder and maker is God."[12]

The passage of Scripture goes on to reveal the keys to living lives of faith, the keys to having victory in our lives, victory over any obstacles and trials we may face. We are told that we should be laying aside those things that will slow us down in our Christian life, and laying aside the sin which can easily trap us, and that we should be running the race with endurance, "looking unto Jesus."[13] Those three words, "looking unto Jesus" are everything. They are absolutely essential. That word, "looking" in the original language means "to continually stare with awe and admiration." It is the only place in the New Testament

> **Those three words, "looking unto Jesus" are everything. They are absolutely essential.**

where it is used. The passage says we should be "looking unto Jesus... who for the joy that was set before Him endured the cross... and has sat down at the right hand of the throne of God."[14]

Jesus endured the incredible humiliation, torture and suffering of crucifixion on the cross. He became "sin,"[15] He

---

[10] Hebrews 10:34
[11] Hebrews 11:16 (NASB)
[12] Hebrews 11:10
[13] Hebrews 12:2
[14] Hebrews 12:2
[15] 2 Corinthians 5:21

became "a curse,"[16] and He was crushed by His own Father.[17] And He endured it all "for the joy that was set before Him." In other words, Jesus was able to endure the cross by looking at the future joy. What was that joy? What was it that gave Him the motivation? He wanted to please and glorify God by freeing you and me from the power and penalty of our sin and to bring us to Heaven where we will live with Him forever. He "has sat down at the right hand of the throne of God." He is now in Heaven. This passage of Scripture is the icing on the cake, the tallest mountain peak, the highest height of truth in the entire Bible on the subject of living out our Christian faith. After going through example after example throughout History of people walking by faith, the writer of the book of Hebrews gives us the greatest example- Jesus Christ. And the writer tells us why Jesus came to this earth and why He died on the cross- the incentive, the motivation for it all. Here, the Almighty God gives us the key to living the Christian life, the

> The Apostle Paul said the "enemies of the cross of Christ...set their mind on earthly things," but "our citizenship is in heaven, from which we... eagerly wait" for Jesus.

key to running the race- he tells us we should be continually fixing our eyes on Jesus, who looked toward the joy of Heaven, and who is now in Heaven.

Over and over again in the Bible, we are told about the forward focus of faith. The Apostle Paul said the "enemies of the cross of Christ...set their mind on earthly things."[18] But Paul commended believers for looking forward- for waiting for Jesus to come from Heaven.[19] He said, "Our citizenship is in heaven, from which we also eagerly wait for the Savior, the Lord Jesus Christ."[20] Paul says we should be "eagerly" waiting

---

[16] Galatians 3:13
[17] Isaiah 53:10 (NASB)
[18] Philippians 3:18-19
[19] 1 Thessalonians 1:9-10
[20] Philippians 3:20

for Jesus. Does that describe your life- "Eagerly waiting for Jesus to come"? When we meet the Christian Dalits who are so excited about the Lord and about going to Heaven, and we ask, "What do they have that we don't? How do they get such joy?" The answer has to do with focus. A lot of their present joy comes from looking to their future joy. Like Jesus, who for the joy set before Him, endured the cross, the Christian Dalits, for the joy set before them, endure the difficulties in this life with joy.

I was privileged to spend time with some Christian Dalits and I quickly realized that the people I thought were the poorest people on earth, are actually some of the richest. I envied what they have. There is no money, no treasure, nothing on earth that can buy the joy these precious brothers and sisters in Christ have. They have tremendous joy, not because they had nothing and now they have *something*

> They have tremendous joy, not because they had nothing and now they have something (Jesus and Heaven). They have tremendous joy because they had nothing and now they have everything (Jesus and Heaven)!

(Jesus and Heaven). They have tremendous joy because they had nothing and now they have *everything* (Jesus and Heaven)!

Scripture tells us, "Set your mind on things above, not on things on the earth."[21] Sadly, many of us think so much about the things of this world; that we hardly ever think about the world to come. But it is the thinking about the things of eternity, the Lord and Heaven, that will give us the joy we long for in this life.

Hugh

A few years ago, Hugh, my father-in-law, noticed that a spot on his head was sore. He went to a doctor and was

---

[21] Colossians 3:2

diagnosed with terminal brain cancer. The cancer grew quickly and within a short time, he was admitted to a hospital. My wife, Doreen, and I travelled back to Hawaii from Texas where we were living. We got to visit with Hugh and it was a blessing to see that he was trusting in God. He was at peace, knowing where he was going to spend eternity.

I had to fly back to Texas and about a week later, while I was between flights at the airport in Chicago, I happened to call Doreen to see how Hugh was doing. Tim, our brother-in-law, had talked with Hugh the night before, and reassured him that since he was trusting in Jesus, he was going to be in Heaven soon. As I sat there in the crowded gate area, waiting for my flight, Doreen and I talked. She said Hugh was no longer able to eat or talk and his health was deteriorating. We talked about the fact that he was going to be with the Lord, but Doreen said he seemed to be fighting to stay alive. It seemed that being face to face with death; he was experiencing anxiety. I asked Doreen to put the phone up to his ear so I could talk to him. She did and I talked to Hugh for a few moments. I told him that he didn't need to be afraid of death. I said, "Hugh, Jesus loves you so much. He died for your sins. You have nothing to be afraid of. You can let yourself go and He will take you to Heaven." Immediately after I said that, Doreen was back on the phone. She spoke quickly. "Something's happening to Dad! I need to hang up the phone. I'll call you back."

A few minutes later, Doreen called me back. Hugh had gone to Heaven. I sat there stunned. Hugh had listened to me and stopped fighting to stay alive and the Lord took him Home. I was excited for Hugh. He's now in the presence of God, in fullness of joy. He's experiencing joy like I've never known it. I was excited for him, but then I thought, "Wow. He got there first! He's in Heaven but I'm still here!" I thought, "It's too bad I couldn't have been holding his hand and gone with him." I

> **Hugh made his flight right on time. I'm still waiting for mine.**

know it doesn't work that way. His body was still here but his spirit was with God. Hugh made his flight right on time. I'm still waiting for mine.

Hugh is now on the other side. He is no longer living by faith. He's living by sight. He sees the Lord face to face and is in absolute bliss, absolute joy. He has no pain, no sorrow, he'll never suffer again, and after I take my last breath, I'll be there with him. That's the distance between our life here, and Heaven- one breath. Every one of us who are trusting in the Lord will one day breathe our last breath and then, in an instant, we will take a flight and we will be in His presence, in the glory of Heaven. As the Apostle Paul said, we would rather "be absent from the body and to be present with the Lord."[22]

Caught Up

Speaking of taking a flight and being absent from the body and being present with the Lord, you and I are living in very exciting times. As we know, life is short- we are going to be in Heaven soon. We don't know which day may be our last one. But in addition to that, there is a wonderful event that could happen any moment now. Even without us growing even one day older, or having a heart attack or stroke, or being in an accident that costs us our life, we could go to Heaven today. "How?" you might ask. We've probably all heard of "the rapture" of the church.

The Bible clearly describes what will happen at "the end of the age," when Jesus comes back to judge the earth. There are quite a few great books written on prophecy that detail the many predictions in the Bible that pertain to "the last days" that are being fulfilled in our lifetime (such as the re-establishment of the nation of Israel, nations surrounding Israel preparing to attack, and the forming of a global, one-world government). We are definitely living in the last days. The "great tribulation," (a time of tremendous suffering) will

---

[22] 2 Corinthians 5:8

precede the second coming of Christ. But as Christians, we are not looking forward to the "great tribulation." We are looking forward to an event which is quite different than the "hour of trial which shall come upon the whole world, to test those who dwell on the earth."[23]

Paul said, "For the Lord Himself will descend from heaven with a shout, with the voice of an archangel, and with the trumpet of God. And the dead in Christ will rise first. Then we who are alive and remain shall be caught up together with them in the clouds to meet the Lord in the air. And thus we shall always be with the Lord."[24] Jesus will come down from Heaven at the sound of the trumpet of God. Christians who are living on the earth will be "caught up" to be with Him. That's awesome. An entire generation of Christians will be taken to Heaven without having to die first. Like Enoch, who "walked with God; and he was not, for God took him."[25] The writer of Hebrews says, "Enoch was taken away so that he did not see death, 'and was not found, because God had taken him.'"[26] And like Elijah, who was taken up suddenly into Heaven in a chariot of fire,[27] we may be "caught up," snatched away from the earth by the Lord- "raptured."

> **An entire generation of Christians will be taken to Heaven without having to die first- like Enoch, who "walked with God; and he was not, for God took him."**

Paul said, "We shall not all sleep, but we shall all be changed in a moment, in the twinkling of an eye, at the last trumpet. For the trumpet will sound, and the dead will be raised incorruptible, and we shall be changed. For this

---

[23] Revelation 3:10

[24] 1 Thessalonians.4:16-17

[25] Genesis 5:24

[26] Hebrews 11:5

[27] 2 Kings 2:10-12

corruptible must put on incorruption, and this mortal must put on immortality."[28] So Paul says, "we shall not all sleep."

Not all Christians will have to experience death- some of us will be going immediately from living here on earth, to being in the presence of the Lord. We will be changed- "metamorphosed" like a caterpillar and we'll have our new bodies in the twinkling of an eye. That's quick. I've heard skeptics say, "Yeah, but every generation since the time of Christ thought they would be the last generation." That's true, but one of these generations will be right, and it very well could be ours!

> **What some may see as a mistake on the part of the disciples is actually a vital key to living life. Our eager anticipation of the return of the Lord is crucial to our having joy in this life.**

As you read through the New Testament, you see that the disciples thought Jesus could return at any moment. Do you think that's because they were misguided? Or do you think that by God's design, we are supposed to be eagerly expecting His return?

The Apostle Paul says we should be "eagerly waiting for the revelation of our Lord Jesus Christ."[29] And that "our citizenship is in heaven, from which we also eagerly wait for the Savior, the Lord Jesus Christ."[30] Paul says, "But if we hope for what we do not see, we eagerly wait for it with perseverance."[31] What some may see as a mistake on the part of the disciples is actually a vital key to living life. Our eager anticipation of the return of the Lord is crucial to our having joy in this life. And of all the generations that have lived since the time of Christ, we have the most reasons to be "eagerly waiting for the revelation of our Lord Jesus Christ."[32] With

---

[28] 1 Corinthians 15:51-53
[29] 1 Corinthians 1:7
[30] Philippians 3:20
[31] Romans 8:25
[32] 1 Corinthians 1:7

the huge number of "last days" prophecies being fulfilled in our lifetime, the rapture is imminent- it could happen any moment! As Jesus said, "Surely I am coming quickly,"[33] and "be ready, for the Son of Man is coming at an hour you do not expect."[34]

It is a sad reality that just as Jesus predicted, in the last days "the love of many will grow cold."[35] Many of us Christians get so caught up in the things of this world that we rarely think about Jesus' soon return. It should be something we think about constantly and should be a tremendous source of joy and strength for us. We should be "eagerly waiting" for Him. Christians in the first century (many of whom faced tremendous persecution) often greeted each other by saying, "Maranatha,"[36] which could be translated as "The Lord is coming," or "Come, O Lord." It was a reminder that at any moment, the Lord could come to get us. Maranatha! We're going Home!

One More Breath

We don't know when our last breath will be. You and I could be with the Lord before you finish reading this sentence, or it could be 60 years from now, but whenever that moment comes, it will come in an instant and then we will be in absolute bliss. It is so close. This life is a vapor- a puff of smoke! Like King David, we should all pray, "LORD, make me to know my end and what is the extent of my days; Let me know how transient I am."[37] Every one of us has a transient life, a fleeting life, a short and fragile life. We are just passing through. We're just camping here for a few days, and then we get to go Home. And the prize we receive for trusting in Jesus

---

[33] Revelation 22:20
[34] Luke 12:40
[35] Matthew 24:12
[36] 1 Corinthians 16:22
[37] Psalm 39:4 (NASB)

and for eagerly waiting for Him[38] will make a $10 million sweepstakes prize look like sawdust. If we will choose to keep our eyes on the prize, we can have a tremendous amount of joy as we finish up these few short days on this earth. Heaven is going to be awesome and if we focus on that truth, it will radically change our lives. And as we'll see in the next chapter, knowing for sure where you are going will make all the difference in the world.

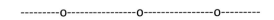

Heavenly Father, Thank You for the promise of Heaven. Thank You for promising to give me a new body- a strong, perfect body that will live forever. Please help me to know that time is short. Help me to know how much better eternal things are, than the temporary things of this world. Make me like those triumphant saints mentioned in Hebrews Chapter 11, who thought about Heaven so much that it radically changed their lives here on earth. Jesus, please help me to continually fix my eyes on You and Heaven as I live my life. Thank You for loving me. Maranatha! Come, Lord Jesus! In Your name I pray, Amen.

---

[38] Luke 12:37; 2 Timothy 4:8

4

Where Are You Going?

"...he was looking for the city which has foundations, whose architect and builder is God."
- Hebrews 11:10

You may have known Jesus for many years, a short time, or maybe you haven't yet made that decision to receive Christ. Regardless of your relationship with God, you may not know with 100% absolute certainty whether or not you will go to Heaven. You might think, "Hmm, Heaven sounds awesome and I think I'm going there after this life, but I'm not 100% absolutely sure, so it's kind of hard for me to get too excited about it." Well, you know what? You can know for sure- today.

Knowing we will go to Heaven is vital. We are in a great spiritual war. The enemy of our souls wants to destroy our lives. And just as a helmet is a critical element of a warrior's armor, we need to be armed with the "helmet of salvation."[1] We need to know that we know that we are saved from the coming judgement. If we have doubts, the enemy can easily discourage us and rob us of joy- making us vulnerable to his attacks and making us innefective as Christians. This chapter may seem basic to some, but it is critical that we are fully convinced of the absolute certainty of our salvation.

Our Problem

The Bible tells us that God is love.[2] This is an amazing truth. The God who created the entire universe- the sun,

---

[1] Ephesians 6:17
[2] 1 John 4:8

moon, earth and stars; the God who made light, colors, sunsets, rainbows, warmth, the coolness of night, gentle breezes, laughter and joy, is the God who is love. He created every good thing that has been created. His desire is that you and I both would spend eternity (after this life) in Heaven (and on the new earth). You may already know this, but there is a problem with God wanting you and me to go to Heaven- we don't deserve to be there.

Many people think that since God is a God of love, He will overlook people's sins, and allow everyone into Heaven. The truth is that God is not only a God of love; He is also perfectly good- absolutely good. Since God is absolutely good, it means He is also absolutely fair- perfectly just. When we get to the end of our lives, every one of us will be judged by God. As the writer of the book of Hebrews says, "it is appointed for men to die once, but after this the judgment."[3] Many people think they are good enough to go to Heaven.

> If we compare ourselves to other people, our sins don't look so bad. But if we compare our lives to the standard of absolute goodness, we quickly see that we all fall far short of true goodness.

They think that on Judgment Day, their good deeds will outweigh their bad deeds. Can you imagine a murderer standing in a courtroom in front of a judge and saying something like, "Well, your honor, I murdered those 10 people, but I've also done a lot of good things, too. I think that since you are a good judge, you will let me go free." The judge might respond with something like, "You are right. I am a good judge, and that is exactly why I am going to see to it that you pay the penalty for your crimes."

We tend to judge things by our own standards. God judges absolutely rightly. You may have heard of the comparison to sheep. When you look at a herd of sheep standing on a hillside of green grass, the sheep look very clean

---
[3] Hebrews 9:27

and white- they look spotless. But if it was to snow and you were to look at those same sheep half an hour later, they would look brown and dirty compared to the perfectly white snow. It's the same with our sins. If we compare ourselves to other people, our sins don't look so bad. We all know people who are a lot worse than we are- like Adolph Hitler or maybe our neighbors. But if we compare our lives to the standard of absolute goodness, we quickly see that we all fall far short of true goodness. On Judgment Day, we would all look like the dirty sheep on a hillside of perfectly white snow.

A Perfect Standard

Have you ever told a lie? Yes? I have, too. Do you know what that makes us? Liars. And liars deserve to be in the lake of fire.[4] Have you ever been angry with someone without an absolutely perfect reason? If you have, Jesus said that it's as if you have committed murder in your heart.[5] If you are driving down the street and someone cuts in front of you and you think, "Oh! I could kill that guy!" In your heart, you *did* just kill him. We've just looked at a couple of our sins and already we are guilty, and are liars and murderers at heart. Do you think liars and murderers deserve to go to Heaven for eternity? Don't think too hard to come up with the answer to that question. The answer is simple- No. Liars and murderers do not deserve to be in absolute joy and bliss in Heaven for eternity- we deserve God's absolute Judgment.

Let me ask you a question. Adolf Hitler was responsible for the torture and murder of millions of people- men, women and children. Do you think since God is good and loving, that He will say to Adolf Hitler, "You are guilty of torturing and murdering millions of people but since I am loving, it's no problem. Come on into eternal joy in Heaven forever." No, that's not what God will say. He will judge Adolph Hitler for every single sin he ever committed.

---

[4] Revelation 21:8
[5] Matthew 5:21-22

On Judgment Day, you and I will stand before God as liars and murderers (and we are guilty of many other sins as well[6]) and we will pay for every sinful thought, word and action we have ever done- *unless* someone else pays the penalty for us. Well, I've got good news for you, in fact it's "good news of happiness."[7] You probably know this already-Jesus already paid the penalty for your sins. He suffered so you don't have to. By repenting (changing your mind and being willing to turn) from your sins and receiving Him as your Lord and Savior, your sins are forgiven- every single one of them- past, present and future. The penalty for your sins has been paid in full.[8]

For many of us, that is an old truth- we've known it for years. But whether we have just received Jesus recently, or have been believers for decades, that truth can be a difficult one for us to really take to heart. Every one of us has a conscience. We know it is fair for us to pay a penalty for our sins. For example, if someone steals money, they should have to pay it back. If someone burns down their neighbor's house, they should have to pay restitution. We all have a sense of justice, a sense of fairness. God has given every one of us a conscience.

Strat the Sinner

I had been a Christian for about a year and a half. I was going to church on Sundays and was also going to church on Wednesday nights. I would tell people about God when it seemed like a good opportunity to talk about Him. I even carried around Gospel tracts in my pocket, (brochures) that had lots of reasons why people should receive Jesus as their Lord and Savior. I was a "good" Christian.

---

[6] You can see this clearly if you examine your life in light of the 10 Commandments found in Exodus 20:3-17.

[7] Isaiah 52:7 (NASB)

[8] On the cross, Jesus said "Tetelestai," which can be translated as "It is finished" or "paid in full." See John 19:30

I started to think God loved me because I was on His side. I was going to church and doing good things. I thought, "Of course, He should love me." Well, one day I was tempted to commit a particular sin. It was something I knew the Bible says is wrong. As I thought about committing this sin, I thought, "This is wrong. I shouldn't do it, and I know the Bible says it's sin." I went ahead and did it anyway. Afterwards, I felt guilty. It was rebellion against God. I had absolutely no excuse in the world for committing that sin.

I prayed to God, "Lord, I knew that was a sin. I knew it before I did it and I did it anyway. There is no reason why You should forgive me, but I am asking You to forgive me anyway." I am not one of those people who have lots of miraculous, supernatural experiences with God, but as those words finished coming out of my mouth, God touched me. It was as if His finger reached down out of Heaven and touched the top of my head. I was flooded from head to toe with a powerful sense of God's love. It was as if God said to me a million times in a split second, "I love you. I love you. I love you." I was overwhelmed. I couldn't believe it. I thought, "Who are You, God? How could You love *me* so much?" Here I was, immediately after committing a sin against God, and He was there telling me He loves me. It was as if He said to me, "You don't understand, Strat. I don't love you because of who you are or because you are trying to be good. I love you because of who I am."

Jacob the Sinner

We have probably all heard of Abraham, Isaac and Jacob. Abraham is called the father of faith. His son Isaac was a wonderful man of God. Isaac's son, Jacob, is also well-known to students of the Bible. One of the many wonderful things about the Bible is that it tells the truth about people. It doesn't paint an inaccurate picture of anyone. The name "Jacob" means "heel catcher" or "supplanter" (which means to take the place of another, through force, scheming, or strategy).

Jacob was born the twin brother of Esau, and as Esau came out of his mother's womb, Jacob was still inside, reaching out, trying to grab hold of his brother's heel. He didn't want his brother to be born first. That's the kind of guy he was- always wanting to get something that wasn't rightfully his. I heard one Bible teacher define Jacob's name as "dirty, sneaky, thief."

Then God got a hold of Jacob's life. God changed his life and his attitude toward life and when He did, He gave Jacob a new name. He said, "Your name shall no longer be called Jacob, but Israel."[9] Israel means "governed by God," or "God prevails." Jacob was no longer to be a dirty, sneaky thief; he was to be governed by God.

It's fascinating that numerous times in the Bible, God calls Himself, "The God of Abraham, Isaac and Jacob," but never once calls Himself, "The God of Abraham, Isaac and Israel." Since God changed Jacob's name to Israel, don't you think it would sound better for God to point out that He is the God of Israel (governed by God), rather than the God of Jacob (the thief)? Why wouldn't God use the name Israel instead of Jacob?

By telling us that He is the God of Jacob, God reminds us repeatedly, that He is the God of the imperfect, the undeserving, the "dirty, sneaky thieves." "While we were still sinners, Christ died for us."[10] God loves you. And He doesn't love you because you are good or because you are trying to be good. He loves you because of who He is- He is the God who is gracious and merciful.

Chosen

"He chose us in Him before the foundation of the world."[11] God chose you to be adopted as His child before He

---

[9] Genesis 32:28

[10] Romans 5:8

[11] Ephesians 1:4

created the world. You were "predestined" to be adopted.[12] It wasn't because He needed you for anything. He didn't choose you because you are lovable or because you are a good person.[13] As He tells us, "There is none righteous, no, not one... There is none good, no, not one."[14] Compared to other people, we may think we are good, but compared to God's absolute standard of holiness and goodness, there is not one truly good person.

A few years ago, Doreen and I got to visit the Grand Canyon for the first time. As I walked up to the edge of the canyon, my jaw almost dropped open. I could only say one thing- "Wow!" It brought tears to my eyes. If you've been there, you know that pictures can't capture the incredible size and beauty of the canyon. The Grand Canyon is about 10 miles across. If I was to try to jump across the Grand Canyon, obviously, I would fall far short. I'd probably only be able to jump 8 or 10 feet toward the other side. If the world's greatest athlete tried to run up to the edge of the Grand Canyon and jump across, he or she might be able to jump 25 or 30 feet. Since the Grand Canyon is 10 miles across, they wouldn't stand a chance of making it to the other side.

If however, someone came by in a helicopter and picked the world's greatest athlete and myself up and flew us to the other side of the canyon and dropped us off, it would be easy for us both to get across. All we would need to do is to sit down and enjoy the ride. That's sort of like trying to be good enough for God, or trying to earn His love. It's like He is the one coming by in the helicopter and saying, "Have a seat." For some reason, we still feel the need to try to make it on our own. "God, I might be able to jump 20 feet. If you give me some time to work at it, maybe if I train real hard, I will be able to jump 30 feet! Will you love me if I do?" It's 10 miles across! What are we thinking?!

---

12 Ephesians 1:4-5
13 Titus 3:4-5
14 Romans 3:10,12

Trying to please God should not be an effort to earn God's love; it should be a response to His love. As the Apostle John wrote, "We love Him because he first loved us."[15] He chose us because of who He is- not because of how special or lovable we are. If God chose you because of how lovable you are; you

> **If God chose you because of how lovable you are; you would need to make sure you stay lovable in order for Him to continue to love you. He chose you because He is love.**

would need to make sure you stay lovable in order for Him to continue to love you. He chose you because He is love[16]- He is a God of mercy and grace and He delights in showing mercy to those who don't deserve it- that's us.

What About Good Works?

Many people think we need to do good works in order to earn a place in Heaven. Paul tells us, "For by grace you have been saved through faith, and that not of yourselves; it is the gift of God, not of works, lest anyone should boast."[17] The Bible is absolutely clear. First, Paul says, "you have been saved," not "you will be saved if..." There is a big difference between someone saying "You have become pregnant," (past tense) and someone saying, "You will become pregnant if..." (future tense). When it comes to our salvation, the "past tense" of the statement, "You have been saved," makes all the difference in the world.

If you have put your trust in Jesus, you already have been saved from the penalty of your sins. You can rejoice- your name is already written in Heaven![18] Again, Paul says "In Him you also trusted, (past tense) after you heard the word of truth, the gospel of your salvation; in whom also, having believed, (past tense) you were sealed (past tense) with the

---

[15] 1 John 4:19

[16] 1 John 4:16

[17] Ephesians 2:8-9

[18] Luke 10:20

Holy Spirit of promise."[19] Is God a liar? Will He break His promises? Absolutely not! And if He says you are "sealed with the Holy Spirit of promise," and are saved- you are saved! We should never make the mistake of calling God a liar! If we want to live a life of joy, this is a critical truth to know. If you are trusting in Christ, you already have salvation!

Notice that Paul clearly says we are not saved by works- our salvation is a "gift of God." We don't figure out faith. We don't earn it. We simply believe (have faith in) what God has done for us. "But when the kindness and the love of God our Savior toward man appeared, not by works of righteousness which we have done, but according to His mercy He saved us... "[20] As Paul says, God saved us because of His kindness, love and mercy.

The Apostle Paul also says, "work out your own salvation with fear and trembling; for it is God who works in you both to will and to do for His good pleasure."[21] Notice that he says we should "work out" our salvation. He doesn't say we should "work for" our salvation. This is critical- we are "working out" our salvation, not "working for"

> **If we believe there are works we need to do in order to earn salvation, we will never "rest in God" and will never live a life of joy.**

it. We do good works because we already have salvation, not in order to earn it. If we believe there are works we need to do in order to earn salvation, we will never "rest in God" and we will never live a life of joy.

This is a very important truth of Christianity. When Jesus died on the cross, He said, "It is finished," which also could be translated as "Paid in full."[22] Your debts have been paid in full because you have put your trust in Jesus and His righteousness has already been credited to your account.

---

[19] Ephesians 1:13
[20] Titus 3:4-5
[21] Philippians 2:12-13
[22] John 19:30

It's Who He Is

We will never be good enough to deserve God's love. He loves us because He wants to love us, it's who He is- He is a loving God. It's essential that you and I realize that. Even as Christians, we can go through life trying to be good enough for God. Give it up. You and I will never be good enough to deserve to go to Heaven. We'll never be good enough to measure up to His perfect standard- absolute holiness. Jesus suffered and died for you and me because we are sinners, not because we are good.

Are You Good Enough?

When you think about it, it would be impossible to make sense out of us having to be good enough to go to Heaven. How many good works would a person have to do to be good enough to deserve to go to Heaven- 500, 1,000? Maybe the number would be 4,274? It's rediculous. What if one person did the 4,274 required good works and another person only did 4,273? Would they deserve to go to Hell because they were one good work short? Or might the determining factor be the number of sins a person commits? What if the number was 1,000 and one person committed 1,000 sins but another only committed 999? Would the first person deserve Hell, but the second person deserve Heaven? In truth, there is a number of sins that a person commits that makes them deserving of Judgment and of separation from a perfect, Holy God- one. How many people do you have to murder to be a murderer? One. And every single one of us has far exceeeded our quota of one murder. God saves us because of His goodness, not ours.

If I've learned two things in my 25 years of being a Christian, one is how much God loves me, and the other is how much of a sinner I am. I fall short every day, and so do you,[23] but God chose you. He loves you. And He doesn't just

---

[23] 1 John 1:8

love you as a member of the human race. It's not like He says, "Well, I love you because I love everyone and I guess that includes you, too." No. He loves you personally. He chose you as an individual before He created the world. He was thinking of you. He knew your name long before anyone else ever thought of it.

King David wrote, "How precious also are Your thoughts to me, O God! How great is the sum of them! If I should count them, they would be more in number than the sand."[24] Have you ever thought about how many grains of sand there are in the world? If you counted one grain of sand every second, it would take hundreds of billions of years to count them all. That's how many thoughts God thought toward David, and guess what? That's how many thoughts He thinks towards you as well. That's how much God loves you. Jesus, who was God in human flesh, came to this earth to suffer and die to pay the penalty for your sins. Do we even begin to grasp the magnitude of that statement? It's no wonder that Paul prayed that we would "be able to comprehend with all the saints what is the width and length and depth and height- to know the love of Christ which passes knowledge."[25]

This is an extremely important point in this book. If you don't think God loves you, not just everyone, but *you*, I encourage you to put this book down for a little while right now and pray about it. Ask God to reveal to you, how much He loves you. If you want to live a life of joy, it is critical that you realize that God loves YOU. He chose you before He created the world because He wants to spend eternity in Heaven with YOU.

How Can You Know?

You might ask, "How do I know that God chose me? Maybe I'm mistaken and I think I'm a follower of Jesus but I'm really not." That's a good question. The way you know

---

[24] Psalm139:17-18
[25] Ephesians 3:18-19

God has chosen you, is that you have chosen Him. Your desire to receive Jesus as your Lord and Savior is a result of God putting that desire in your heart.[26] Salvation is a gift of God.[27] If you have chosen to put your faith in Jesus Christ, you can be certain that He has chosen you, because Jesus said He chose you- He clearly said, "No one can come to Me unless the Father who sent Me draws him."[28] If you have chosen Him, you can be abolutely sure He has chosen you!

Nobody is going to be able to stand in Heaven and say anything like, "Well, I was smart enough to figure out that God is real and that Jesus died for me." And nobody will be saying, "There was something good in me that attracted God to me." No, we will all be saying, "Blessing and honor and glory and power be to Him who sits on the throne, and to the Lamb, forever and ever!"[29] "Salvation is of the Lord."[30] Like someone who wants to get to the other side of the Grand Canyon, we don't stand a chance on our own, but like the helicopter pilot who comes along, God says, "Have a seat." We put our trust in the work that Jesus finished on the cross- He paid your penalty because He loves you.

Another great thing about the Bible is that the important truths are laid out so clearly. People ask, "How can I know I have eternal life and that I'm going to Heaven?" The Bible tells us that "God has given us eternal life, and this life is in His Son. He who has the Son has life; he who does not have the Son of God does not have life."[31] Do you have the Son? Have you received Jesus as your Lord and Savior? We shouldn't go through life just hoping we are going to Heaven in the same way that we might be hoping we won't ever get sick. The promises of God are all 100% absolutely

---

[26] John 6:44
[27] Ephesians 2:8
[28] John 6:44
[29] Revelation 5:14
[30] Jonah 2:9
[31] 1 John 5:11-12

trustworthy. "He who has the Son has life." If we have Jesus as our Lord and Savior, we have eternal life. We don't have to just hope we will go to Heaven one day; we can know we are going to Heaven because God said we are. Jesus said, "And if I go and prepare a place for you, I will come again and receive you to Myself; that where I am, there you may be also."[32] When the Bible speaks of our Heavenly hope, it speaks of the "hope of eternal life which God, who cannot lie, promised before time began."[33]

Maybe there is a little part in all of us that keeps wondering, "Have I done enough to be able to go to Heaven?" In case you don't know this- there are two things that are necessary for you to get to Heaven. Of course, Jesus said it best- "Repent, and believe in the gospel."[34] First, we must "repent" (change our mind about our sin) and secondly, we must "believe in the Gospel" (as Paul says, the Gospel is "that Christ died for our sins according to the Scriptures, and that He was buried, and that He rose again the third day..."[35]). First- Have you repented (changed your mind about your sin)? Are you willing to forsake your sins and follow Jesus as your Lord? Second- Do you believe that He died for your sins and rose again on the third day? If you answer yes to those two questions, then according the words of the Living God, you are saved.

Of course, the reason that some people wonder if they are saved, is because they aren't. They may own a Bible, go to church and spend time with Christians. Maybe they've even "prayed the sinner's prayer." But in order to be saved you must repent and receive Jesus as your Lord and Savior. You must be born again.[36] When you do that, your life will change.

---

[32] John 14:3

[33] Titus 1:2

[34] Mark 1:15; See also Matthew 3:2;4:17; Mark 6:12; Luke 13:3; Acts 3:19, 17:30, 26:20

[35] 1 Corinthians 15:3-4

[36] John 3:3; John 1:12

Will there be bright lights and whistles? Will God speak to you with a voice of thunder? Probably not, but you will notice God working in your life- you will notice that you are not content to be living in sin anymore, and you will have a desire to do what God wants you to do.[37] If you have never repented and received Jesus as your Lord and Savior- pray and do it now.

The Apostle John tells us, "But as many as received Him, to them He gave the right to become children of God, to those who believe in His name."[38] Because we have received Jesus Christ and have put our trust (believe) in Him, we are adopted as children of God and will live with Him forever. We don't just hope we will be going to Heaven- we know we will be.

Dealing With Doubt

It is very common for us Christians to doubt our salvation. One day we think God has saved us and that we will be going to Heaven, and the next day we don't feel like we are good enough. This is one of the biggest joy-stealers in the Christian life. This is something that was a problem for me for many years. It didn't matter how often I went to church, prayed, read my Bible or how good I tried to be. I had this nagging, recurring thought, "What if I'm not really a Christian? What if I get to the end of my life and find out I wasn't following Jesus enough?"

Nobody follows Jesus perfectly. Think of the most committed Christian you have met or ever heard of. If you were to ask them how perfectly they follow Jesus, they would probably be very quick to admit they fall far short. The Bible says, "If we say that we have no sin, we deceive ourselves, and the truth is not in us."[39] Every one of us falls short. The key to having assurance of our salvation is not in how perfectly we follow Jesus. The key is that we are seeking to follow Him and trust Him as our Lord. The key is in our intention. Do you

---

[37] 1 John 1:6-9; 2:3-6

[38] John 1:12

[39] 1 John 1:8

seek to follow Him as Lord? The Apostle Paul tells us, "if you confess with your mouth the Lord Jesus and believe in your heart that God has raised Him from the dead, you will be saved... For 'whoever calls on the name of the LORD shall be saved.'"[40] Whoever calls on the name of the Lord shall be saved- period. Again, if you have not received Jesus as your Lord and Savior; call on Him right now. Surrender to the God who loves you and who suffered and died on the cross and then rose again from the dead- for you.

We can struggle with the assurance of our salvation for years, or we can take our focus off of ourselves and put it on Jesus, and find rest. The Bible is perfectly clear- "God has given us eternal life, and this life is in His Son. He who has the Son has life; he who does not have the Son of God does not have life. These things I have written to you who believe in the name of the Son of God,

> **We can struggle with the assurance of our salvation for years, or we can take our focus off of ourselves and put it on Jesus, and find rest.**

that you may know that you have eternal life."[41] He says, "that you may know," not "that you may hope." You can know right now that you have eternal life.

If assurance of your salvation is something you struggle with, I encourage you to write down some of the verses mentioned in this chapter, and to read them over and over. Pray about them, meditate on (ponder) them and think about them. It would probably be helpful to memorize some of them as well, so that you can be thinking about them throughout the day, or you might want to carry a piece of paper with the verses written on it, so you can have it handy. When you have a moment, pull it out and read it and pray and think about it. As you do, God will increase your faith and joy. "Faith comes by hearing and hearing by the word of God."[42] As you

---

[40] Romans 10:9,13
[41] 1 John 5:11-13
[42] Romans 10:17

meditate and pray about your relationship with God, He will give you that wonderful "joy and peace in believing."[43]

Knowing where you are going is essential to living a life of joy, and as we will see in the next chapter, so is knowing who you are.

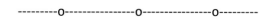

Heavenly Father, Thank You for sending Your Son to come to this earth to suffer and die to pay the penalty for my sins. I know I'm not good enough to deserve to go to Heaven and I am so thankful that You give me eternal life and the promise of Heaven as a gift. Thank You for being a God of love. Thank You for loving me and saving me. Jesus, thank You for dying for me. I surrender to You as my Lord and Savior. Help me to realize that I'm not going to Heaven because of what I do; I'm going to Heaven because of what You already did for me on the cross. Thank You for loving me with an everlasting love. Help me to follow You all the days of my life. I love You. In Your name I pray, Amen.

---

[43] Romans 15:13

5

Are You Rich?

"... our citizenship is in heaven..."
- Philippians 3:20

When I was younger, I used to be envious of people who were born into rich families. I thought, "Think of all the things I could do if I just had lots of money." But many rich people are miserable. Money is no guarantee of happiness. In fact, as Paul writes, "The love of money is a root of all kinds of evil, for which some have strayed from the faith in their greediness, and pierced themselves through with many sorrows."[1] There is nothing wrong with being rich,[2] but there is a lot wrong with being greedy and loving money. Whether we are rich or poor- riches are not the source of true happiness- God is.

Not Getting What We Deserve

But guess what? You and I are already rich! When we received Jesus Christ, we became spiritually connected to Him. We are "in" Christ. Just as your elbow and your head are parts of your body, every Christian is part of the body of Christ (and He is the head of the body). As the Apostle Paul wrote, "we, being many, are one body in Christ"[3] This is not just a figure of speech. One of the things that can bring us great joy in life, is knowing who we really are in Christ. We are spiritually united with each other and with Jesus Christ, the Creator of the universe. So what does that mean?

---

[1] 1 Timothy 6:10
[2] Proverbs 10:4
[3] Romans 12:5

For one thing, it means we are not going to get what we deserve- God's Judgment. It means that our sins have already been judged and paid for on the cross. Jesus became sin for us and the righteousness of Jesus, the righteousness of God, has been credited to our accounts.[4] When we stand before God on Judgment Day, He will see us as perfectly sinless. "There is therefore now no condemnation to those who are in Christ Jesus."[5] We are 100% totally forgiven for every single sin we ever have committed, and ever will commit.

Getting What We Don't Deserve

It also means we will get what we don't deserve- the reward that was due to Jesus for living an absolutely perfect, Holy, others-centered life- we get to go to Heaven and live forever. And not only will we receive Heaven, but we will have God Himself, forever. As King David wrote, "O LORD, You are the portion of my inheritance and my cup."[6] And as the psalmist wrote, "God is the strength of my heart and my portion forever."[7] What could be greater riches than having God Himself, forever? You are a trillion times richer than all of the billionaires in the world put together! And that statement doesn't even scratch the surface of the depths of the riches we have in Christ. Oh, that we could see even a faint glimpse of the magnitude of this truth! We have God!

Paying a Trillion Dollar Debt with a Penny

If you are trusting in Christ, God has already chosen you, accepted you, forgiven you and predestined you for Heaven.[8] It's amazing to realize that eternal life in Heaven with God is a free gift.[9] There's nothing we need to do to be good enough.

---

[4] 2 Corinthians 5:21
[5] Romans 8:1
[6] Psalm 16:5
[7] Psalm 73:26
[8] Ephesians 1:3-7
[9] Romans 5:18: 6:23

Jesus already did it for us. Trying to be good enough is sort of like having someone walk up to you and give you a trillion dollars and then you saying, "Wow! That's amazing! Let me pay you a penny for it." Jesus, God in human flesh, died for you- you could never pay Him back.

Many of the most discouraged, unhappy and frustrated Christians you will ever meet are the ones who are trying to measure up to God's standards, trying to be good enough for God. It results in constant discouragement- "I'm so unworthy. God couldn't possibly love me or approve of me, and if other Christians knew what I say and do, and what goes through my mind, they wouldn't want to have anything to do with me either."

> **You have already earned God's 100% absolute approval- in Christ!**

You have already earned God's 100% absolute approval- in Christ! If you take this to heart, it will be a tremendous source of joy for you. Pray about it. As far as measuring up to God's perfect standard of holiness, you are already absolutely perfect- in Christ.[10] God didn't choose you because you are special; you are special because God chose you.

> **God didn't choose you because you are special; you are special because God chose you.**

Every Spiritual Blessing

We often hear about what we should be doing for God- how we should be giving more money, serving more, praying more, reading the Bible more, or telling more people about Jesus. Unfortunately, some churches really emphasize what we ought to be doing for God. Every time we go to one of these churches, we are reminded that we aren't doing enough for Him. We can live our lives feeling guilty and defeated. The Bible, on the other hand, emphasizes what God has already

---

[10] Hebrews 10:14

done for us. In the New Testament, we are always told about God's love for us, before being told about how we should respond to God. The book of Ephesians is a great example of this. In the beginning of the first chapter, the wonderful truth is given to us- God "has blessed us with every spiritual blessing in the heavenly places in Christ"[11] This is an amazing truth- God has already blessed us with amazing riches in Christ.

For the next three chapters, the book of Ephesians expands on this wonderful truth; verse after verse reveal blessings God has given us. Many books have been written explaining just how wonderful these blessings are. It isn't until the fourth chapter of the book of Ephesians, that it turns a corner and urges us, "therefore... walk worthy of the calling with which you were called."[12]

> We often hear about what we should be doing for God... The Bible on the other hand, emphasizes what God has already done for us.

Here are some of the wonderful spiritual blessings (mentioned in Ephesians) that He has blessed you with- He chose you before He even created the world.[13] And He chose you to stand "holy and without blame," on Judgment Day.[14] That means that not a single sin you have ever committed will be brought before the Judge of the universe on your day of judgment. You will be seen as being absolutely "holy" and perfect because you are "in Christ." He adopted you and accepted you.[15] Isn't that awesome? He chose to adopt you as His child, and Almighty God has accepted you. You don't have to earn His acceptance. He accepted you before He even created the world. He loves you. Jesus shed His blood for you

---

[11] Ephesians 1:3
[12] Ephesians 4:1
[13] Ephesians 1:4
[14] Ephesians 1:4; Jude 24
[15] Ephesians 1:5-6

so that you could be forgiven of your sins.[16] He has given you His Holy Spirit to help you-[17] the Spirit of the Almighty God. Your inheritance in Heaven is guaranteed.[18] Nobody can take it away from you. You are given a sure hope-[19] not just some wishful thinking. The list goes on and on. You might want to prayerfully read the first three chapters of the book of Ephesians sometime in order to meditate (ponder) on the incredible blessings that God has blessed you with.

Knowing Him

Sin cut off mankind's personal relationship with God and because we are united to Christ, we have that relationship with God restored. That alone is worth more than all the riches in the world. We know the Creator of the universe-personally! He is our Father, our Savior, our Comforter and our friend. He loves us. He knows everything and He wants to lead us in the way we should go. And He speaks to us! He's given us His Word- the Bible, and His Holy Spirit to guide us. And we can talk with Him day and night. We don't have to wait in a line like we do when we go to the Post Office or the store. And we don't have to talk to a priest in order to communicate with God.[20] The Creator and sustainer of the universe is always there for us, every moment of every day. It's amazing.

Many of us don't take advantage of the incredible opportunities we have for "times of refreshing"[21] that come from spending time with God. For the first ten years of my Christian life, prayer was kind of an afterthought. On my way out the door to start my day, I would spend a few minutes reading the Bible and talking to God in prayer. I would also

---

[16] Ephesians 1:7
[17] Ephesians 1:13
[18] Ephesians 1:14
[19] Ephesians 1:18
[20] 1 Timothy 2:5
[21] Acts 3:19

pray quick little prayers, a few times during the day. It seemed to help things but there seemed to be something missing in my life.

Every few months, the thought would occur to me, "I should pray more." I would determine to spend more time in prayer. For the next few days, instead of spending 5 or 10 minutes in prayer, I would pray for about 15 minutes, sometimes even 20. After 3 or 4 days of this "extended prayer," I would go back to praying for about 10 minutes a day. About six months later, I would again determine to spend more time in prayer. My prayer time would again increase to about 15 minutes a day, for a few days. This went on for 10 years.

Finally, after hearing someone mention that they pray for an hour a day, I made a decision. I said, "That's it. I am going to set my alarm clock, wake up earlier, and pray for an hour a day." The next day I woke up, got out of bed (that was an important step), and got down on my knees to pray. I prayed for everything: people I knew, my family, countries of the world, my neighbors and my neighbor's dog- everything I could think of. "Has it been an hour?" I looked at my watch, "Oh, it's only been seven minutes! I have 53 minutes to go!" I forced myself to keep praying. It seemed like a long time before my hour of prayer was finally finished. It felt kind of like I was trying to walk in waste deep water- it was a lot of work.

Times of Refreshing

I continued to set my alarm to wake up to pray, and within a few days, I changed the way I was praying. Instead of just praying for a list of things, I would also spend time praising God, worshipping Him, thanking Him, confessing my sins, and trying to allow Him to lead my prayer time. I wouldn't just talk to God- I would also spend time listening for His still, small voice.[22] The hour of prayer started to fly by quickly. Sometimes things would come to mind to pray-things I hadn't ever thought about before. Or Bible verses would come to mind. Sometimes the Lord would speak to me and I would be so tremendously blessed by what He would say. The "times of refreshing" that the Apostle Peter talked about, that come "from the presence of the Lord,"[23] are truly a treasure.

Within about a week of starting to spend more time in prayer, I started to notice my life changing. For one thing, I had more peace throughout the day. The Apostle Paul said to "let the peace of God rule in your hearts,"[24] and spending time with God in prayer is a way for us to develop intimacy with Him, and in the process, experience much more of His peace in our lives. Many times when I would be faced with decisions, it seemed like I had already been prepared for them. Even though I hadn't thought about them before, I believe that in my times of waiting on the Lord in prayer, God was preparing my spirit for the things I was going to face during the day. It helped me to make right decisions. It gave me a lot of peace in situations in which previously, I would have been experiencing stress. It was a great source of joy for me. And I started to see God working through my life in ways I'd never seen before.

Rivers of Living Water

For example, one afternoon (about a week after increasing my time in prayer), I was walking across a parking lot and I felt a sudden, tremendous urge to pray. It was so clear and strong. I had never experienced anything like that before. I started praying as I walked along and about 50 feet further on, I walked past a young woman sitting in a car. I happened to have a few Gospel tracts in my pocket and I

---

[22] 1 Kings 19:12
[23] Acts 3:19
[24] Colossians 3:15

walked up to the window of her car and held out a Gospel tract. "Can I give you something to read?" I asked.

She took the tract, looked at it and said, "I'm definitely going to read this!" I was shocked. For ten years as a Christian, I would carry Gospel tracts in my pocket and pass them out to people. I'm sure God used the tracts to plant seeds in people's hearts, but in 10 years of passing out tracts, never once had I had a response like this girl's. She explained to me that she had just quit her job and was in the process of moving to another state to start a new life. She said her mother told her she needed spiritual counsel. I thought, "Well, I know The Counselor!" I was so blessed to be able to tell her about Jesus and she was very open to hearing about Him.

> As they say, "You can't out give God." As we seek to allow Him to work through our lives, we will be incredibly blessed.

God says, "Unless the Lord builds the house, they labor in vain who build it."[25] We can live our lives in our own strength-trying so hard to make things work out right. Or we can take advantage of the amazing opportunity we have, to have an intimate relationship with the Creator of the universe- our Heavenly Father. Tied in with that, we can be used by Him to bless people's lives. And we can store up treasure in Heaven that will last forever![26] There's no better way to work for the future or to prepare for "retirement." And the joy we get as we see God work through our lives is a joy that is truly a deep, rich treasure. As they say, "You can't out give God," and as we seek to allow Him to work through our lives, we will be incredibly blessed.

---

[25] Psalm 127:1
[26] Matthew 6:19-20

A Big Family

Another one of the riches that we have in Christ is our family. God adopted us as His children,[27] and every Christian in the world is our brother or sister. As a new Christian, I was amazed at my incredible new family. I would talk with people who I'd never met before; people who were very different than I was, but we would have an instant connection. I travelled to other countries and found the same thing. I'd never been to these countries (and I had no natural relatives there) but I already had family there.

When you attend some churches, especially some of the larger ones, it can tend to feel a bit like a movie theater. You walk in, take your seat, and are "entertained" for an hour and a half, and then you go home. But if you spend time with

> **The church is not just something we attend; it is something we are.**

other Christians (especially if it involves conversations about the things of God), you will quickly see the connection we have as believers. The church is not just something we attend; it is something we are.

We are brothers and sisters. As our relationship with our Heavenly Father grows, and our fellowship with other Christians grows deeper, our relationships will (surprisingly quickly) develop to the point where we even would die for a brother or sister if we needed to, and they would be willing to die for us. People who have completely different backgrounds, from different cultures and different races, some of us are poor and some are rich, some are young and some are old- but God makes us one family. Whether or not we realize it, or take advantage of it, we are truly rich with our wonderful big family. If, up to this point, you hadn't realized this, I encourage you not just to attend a church, but to get involved in church, and to pray about attending a home fellowship or regular prayer meeting. Our brothers and sisters in Christ are

---

[27] Ephesians 1:3-5

truly treasures from God, and as we spend time with them, sharing our lives with them, and sharing in spiritual things, we will indeed find riches and joy.

In Time of Need

When I was a little boy and I got into trouble, most of the time it was my fault. I wouldn't want to go to my parents for help because I was scared that if I did, I would get punished. Like when my neighbor, Mark, and I put some plastic toy soldiers into an ashtray on the kitchen floor and lit them on fire. (The soldiers were the losers in a battle.) We were trying to be careful, but we didn't notice that some of the sparks from the fire got onto a dishtowel that was hanging on a wall a few feet away. I happened to glance over and was shocked by the sight- the dishtowel was engulfed in flames. Mark and I tried a few things to extinguish the fire and finally, after filling a big pot with water, I doused the flaming towel (and burning wall).

The fire was out, but there was water and ashes all over the floor in the kitchen and dining room, and the wall was black. What did we do? We decided it was time to go for a hike. We walked to a nearby hillside where we could safely avoid any possible consequences for our actions. Needless to say, our "escape" didn't work.

Our natural tendency when we do something wrong is to avoid the authority to which we are accountable. But whether or not our troubles are the result of our own actions, we have a God who we can go to for help. He isn't up in Heaven with a big stick, ready to hit us over the head every time we mess up. He loves us. Jesus is not one "who cannot sympathize with our weaknesses, but One who has been tempted in all things as we are, yet without sin."[28] He knows our weaknesses and our temptations. He understands our failures. He knows we need help and He is always there, ready to help us, and He is

---

[28] Hebrews 4:15 (NASB)

God. He is able to help us in any difficulty in life. "Let us therefore come boldly to the throne of grace, that we may obtain mercy and find grace to help in time of need."[29] What incredible blessings we have as God's children. God Himself, will help us and give us mercy and grace in times of need. The help may not always be what we want, or when we want it, but He will always help us. He knows what we really need, and when. "And my God will supply all your needs according to His riches in glory in Christ Jesus."[30]

We Have Everything

The Apostle Paul tells us that we are "complete in Him."[31] If we have Jesus, we have everything. All joy, hope, peace, love, meaning, purpose, and fulfillment in life comes from Him. What else do we need? As A.W. Tozer wrote, "The man who has God for his treasure has all things in One. Many ordinary treasures may be denied him, or if he is allowed to have them, the enjoyment of them will be so tempered that they will never be necessary to his happiness. Or if he must see them go, one after one, he will scarcely feel a sense of loss, for having the Source of all things he has in One all satisfaction, all pleasure, all delight. Whatever he may lose he has actually lost nothing, for he now has it all in One, and he has it purely, legitimately and forever."[32]

We are truly rich in Christ. The reality is that even though we are rich in Christ, we often don't feel rich. It's sort of like having $100 million in the bank, but never making a withdrawal or writing a check. We can be rich and yet live like we are dirt poor. How can we have the source of all true joy, and yet live lives that are lacking joy? Our joy in this life comes as we abide in faith, hope, and love. What does that

---

[29] Hebrews 4:16
[30] Philippians 4:19 (NASB)
[31] Colossians 2:10
[32] A.W. Tozer, The Pursuit of God, Chapter 1

mean? How can we do that? In the next chapter, we'll see how our faith can be a source of great joy.

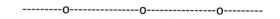

Heavenly Father, Thank You for blessing me so much. Thank You for giving me the greatest riches in the universe- Yourself. Help me to know how truly rich I am in Christ. Thank You for not giving me what I deserve (Your Judgment), and for giving me what I don't deserve (eternal life in Heaven with You). Thank You for seeing me as being perfect in Christ. Thank You for Your Word and Your Holy Spirit. Thank You for loving me, choosing me, adopting me, accepting me, forgiving me, guiding me, comforting me, strengthening me, sustaining me, providing for me, healing me, calling me and for blessing me with every spiritual blessing in Heavenly places in Christ. Thank You for allowing me to know You, and for wanting to give me times of refreshing in Your presence. Thank You that I can talk with You and fellowship with You all day, every day. Thank You for Your promises. Thank You for wanting to use me to help change people's lives for eternity. Thank You for all of my brothers and sisters in Christ. Help me to know how truly blessed I am. I love You. In Jesus' name, Amen.

6

Abiding in Faith

"...the life which I now live in the flesh I live by faith in the Son of God, who loved me and gave Himself for me."
- Galatians 2:20

An Awesome Inheritance

If a stranger knocks on your door tomorrow morning and tells you that you have inherited $50 million, you might think, "Is this for real? Who is this person that just said this to me? It sounds great, but is it really true? Is this person reliable? Did they get the right address?"

Your joy at hearing such a great report would depend on what you think of the reliability of the person giving you the good news. If you believe they are reliable, and they haven't made a case of mistaken identity- that you really are going to receive the inheritance, you would most likely be very excited. Money isn't everything (that's for sure), but you can do a lot with money and it can be something that can bless your life, and other people's lives through you.

If you are convinced that you have this $50 million inheritance coming to you, you would probably be filled with a sense of gratitude- "Wow! I can't believe that someone has decided to bless me so greatly."

You would also start thinking of things you can do with the money. Of course, if you are wanting to please God with your life, a lot of the uses for the money that come to mind would center around what you can do to bless others.

What we have been given, are being given, and will be given by God, is worth infinitely more than $50 million. There is no comparison between the two. Trying to compare them is a little like trying to compare the universe to a grain of sand. At some point, all the money and riches in the world will burn up,[1] and our life on this earth is short, but the riches God has blessed us with (and will bless us with) will last forever and ever.

The joy we experience in our life depends on our faith. In the example of the news of the $50 million inheritance, your joy over the inheritance would depend on three things. Number one: Is the source of the report reliable? Number two: Are you really the intended recipient of this great inheritance? And number three: Your keeping the $50 million inheritance in mind. (If you woke up the morning after hearing about your inheritance and forgot all about it, it wouldn't continue to be a source of joy for you until you remembered it again or received the inheritance.)

In the same way, the joy we derive from our faith is also dependant on those same three things. God's blessings and promises of blessings toward us are amazing. But, like the news of the $50 million, whether or not we rejoice over God's blessings and promises, depends on three things: Number one; Is the report (The Bible and God's Holy Spirit) reliable? Number two; Are His promises really intended for us? And number three; Do we keep His blessings in mind?

We can quickly breeze past those questions and think to ourselves, "Sure, I believe the Bible. I believe those promises are for me, and I think about them sometimes." But the degree to which our faith brings us joy is dependent on the reality of those truths in our lives. Let's more fully consider each one.

Believing God

If you are in a grocery store and someone runs up to you and tells you that a meteorite is falling from the sky and

---

[1] 2 Peter 3:10

heading straight for the store, and that you need to run out of the store immediately, your response would depend on who the person is that is giving you the report. If it is someone you know who has a reputation for telling wild stories and imagining strange things, you probably wouldn't take the warning seriously. Instead, you would probably just feel sorry for the person and continue with your grocery shopping.

If, on the other hand, you knew that the person giving you the warning worked for the National Aeronautics and Space Administration (NASA), and was responsible for monitoring meteorites that approach the earth's atmosphere, you would probably start running to get out of the store. Whether it's great news of inheriting riches, or a warning of a coming disaster, our response to the message depends on the reliability of the messenger.

Consider the Source

I had a personal encounter with Jesus Christ that changed my life (but that's a story for another time), and I received Jesus as my Lord and Savior. About a week later, I started to want to know about the reliability of the Bible. I knew that Jesus had changed my life

> **I examined the evidence for the reliability of the Bible, and to sum up the results of my research in three words-**
> **I was amazed.**

and I wanted to follow Him, but what about the Bible? Is it reliable? I had heard that the Bible can be compared to a game in which people sit in a circle and one person whispers a message to the person next to them. That person whispers the message to the person next to them, and it continues around the circle. By the time the message gets all the way around the circle and the last person speaks it out loud, the message has changed a lot from the message given by the first person in the circle.

I wanted to know, "Can we trust the Bible? Has it changed from when it was originally written? Is it really a book from

God?" I started examining the evidence for the reliability of the Bible, and to sum up the results of my research in three words- I was amazed. I read books like *The New Evidence that Demands a Verdict*, by Josh McDowell, that examine the reliability of the Bible and the Christian faith, and *A General Introduction to the Bible*, by Norman Geisler and William Nix, about how we got our Bible and how we can know it was copied accurately. The evidence for the Christian faith and the reliability of the Bible, are absolutely overwhelming.

What a Book

The Bible is a book like no other book. The Bible is filled with wisdom and truth that can change our lives for eternity, and beyond that, the evidence for the reliability of the Bible makes the Bible rise far above any other book ever written. While a number of books and writings claim to speak for God, neither the Koran, the Hindu Vedas, the Book of Mormon, the Tao-te-ching, the New World Translation of the Watchtower Society, nor any other book or sacred writing, can stand the tests that the Bible can.

One of the many amazing things about the Bible is prophecy. In the Bible, God in effect says, "This is how you'll know I am speaking to you. I will tell you the future in advance." In Isaiah 46:9-10, God says, "...For I am God, and there is no other; I am God, and there is none like Me, declaring the end from the beginning, and from ancient times things that are not yet done..." There are about 2,500 predictions (prophecies) in the Bible. About 2,000 of them have already come to pass, exactly as the Bible predicted they would, and the other 500 or so, predict events that are still in the future. More than one-fourth of the verses in the Bible are prophecy. All it would take is for one of those prophecies to be wrong, and people could rightly question the reliability of the

> In the Bible, God in effect says, "This is how you'll know I am speaking to you. I will tell you the future in advance."

Bible- but there never has been even one wrong prophecy. In fact, many people who have examined the Bible, trying to find mistakes or false prophecies in order to discredit Christianity, have become Christians because the Bible is so amazingly reliable.

What a Nation

Some examples of the Bible's many amazing prophecies involve the Nation of Israel. In the Bible, God said (because of their disobedience to God) the people of Israel would be scattered among the nations, saying, "Then the LORD will scatter you among all peoples, from one end of the earth to the other."[2] This prophecy was made 3,000 years ago and came to pass about 1,000 years later, in 70AD. God also described what the lives of the Jewish people would be like, as

> No other people on earth have left their homeland and yet retained their national identity for more than about 100 years. The Jewish people did it for 2,000 years.

they lived scattered among the nations. He said, "And among those nations you shall find no rest, nor shall the sole of your foot have a resting place; but there the LORD will give you a trembling heart, failing eyes, and anguish of soul. Your life shall hang in doubt before you; you shall fear day and night, and have no assurance of life."[3] Sadly, for almost 2,000 years, the Jewish people lived without a homeland, subject to racial prejudice and persecution (Example- Their treatment by Hitler). Those amazing prophecies were perfectly fulfilled.

But God also said, "Therefore behold, the days are coming," says the LORD... I will bring them back into their land which I gave to their fathers."[4] On May 14, 1948, after 2,000 years of being scattered among the nations, Israel again

---

[2] Deuteronomy 28:64, See also Leviticus 26:33, Jeremiah 9:16, Ezekiel 12:15
[3] Deuteronomy 28:65-66
[4] Jeremiah 16:14-15. See also Jeremiah 3:14; 31:8-9, Isaiah 60:8-9, Deuteronomy 30:3, Amos 9:15

became a nation. In all of history, there has never been another nation like Israel. No other people on earth have left their homeland and yet retained their national identity for more than about 100 years. The Jewish people did it for 2,000 years. They were driven out from their homeland and remained scattered around the world and then 2,000 years later, just as God predicted, they returned from all over the world, and Israel again became a nation. This is another one of thousands of perfectly fulfilled Biblical prophecies.

Some of the prophecies about Israel are even being fulfilled in our lifetime. For example, around the year 520BC, God predicted that in the last days (the days in which we are now living), "it shall happen in that day that I will make Jerusalem a very heavy stone for all peoples... "[5] One of the things that makes this prophecy so amazing is that it was made when Jerusalem lay in ruins, so to predict that

> About 2500 years ago, when Jerusalem lay in ruins, God predicted that He would make Israel "a heavy stone for all peoples." That prophecy is being fulfilled in our lifetime.

Israel would become a burden for the nations was quite a claim. Today, Israel is a nation about the size of New Jersey, and has 0.01% of the world's population (less than the population of New Jersey), and yet an amazing number of United Nations resolutions involve Israel. Israel is the object of more emergency sessions at the UN than any other country in the world, and the UN Human Rights Council adopts more resolutions condemning Israel than it does on the rest of the world combined.[6] Israel could very well be the center of the next major war and has indeed become "a very heavy stone for all peoples."

---

[5] Zechariah 12:3
[6] Irwin Cotler, Jerusalem Post, August 15, 2013

What a God

These are just a few of the thousands of prophecies in the Bible. There are approximately 800 prophecies about Jesus Christ in the Bible, and He fulfilled every one of them, except for the ones that will come to pass in the future. He perfectly fulfilled hundreds of prophecies written about the Messiah that were written hundreds of years before He was born. These prophecies predict where and when He would be born,[7] where He would live,[8] what people would say about Him,[9] His rejection by His brethren,[10] that He would do miracles,[11] even the very day that He would enter into Jerusalem was predicted,[12] that His hands and feet would be pierced,[13] (an

> **It was prophesied that Jesus' hands and feet would be pierced. That's an amazing prediction considering the fact that crucifixion wasn't even invented until about 500 years after the prophecy was made.**

amazing prediction considering the fact that crucifixion wasn't even invented until about 500 years after the prophecy was made) that He would die for the sins of the people,[14] that He would be betrayed for 30 pieces of silver,[15] and that He would rise again from the dead[16] (a fact attested to by over 500 eyewitnesses). The list goes on and on. Of the thousands of prophecies in the Bible, not one single prophecy has been wrong. The reason the Bible is such an amazing book, is because it was written by the amazing God. God "breathed"

---

[7] Micah 5:2; Genesis 49:10
[8] Isaiah 9:1-2
[9] Psalm 22:7-8
[10] Isaiah 8:14; Isaiah 53:1-3; Psalm 69:8-9
[11] Isaiah 35:5-6
[12] Daniel 9:24-25
[13] Psalm 22:16; Zechariah 12:10
[14] Isaiah 53:5-12
[15] Zechariah 11:12
[16] Psalm 16:10-11; Isaiah 26:19

His Spirit into the writing of the Bible.[17] We can trust it- absolutely. As Jesus said, "Heaven and earth will pass away, but My words will by no means pass away."[18]

Our faith in God and in the Bible is not a blind faith. Some people like to make fun of Christians and say we believe in Jesus in the same way little children believe in Santa Clause or the Easter Bunny. There is no comparison. The evidence that supports our faith in God and the Bible is tremendous.

Simon Greenleaf was a Royal Professor at Harvard and was instrumental in establishing Harvard Law School. He wrote a 3 volume work titled, *Treatise on the Law of Evidence*, which was a standard textbook in American law schools during the Nineteenth century. For over half a century, his books were used to teach lawyers how to determine what valid evidence is in a court of law, and his work is still considered the greatest single authority on evidence in the entire literature of legal procedure. After being challenged to examine the evidence for Christianity, Mr. Greenleaf, the expert on evidence, set out to disprove the Christian faith. After examining the evidence for himself, Simon Greenleaf became a committed Christian and stated, "When we have this degree of evidence, it is unreasonable to require more."[19]

> "When we have this degree of evidence, it is unreasonable to require more." - Simon Greenleaf (Author of *Treatise on the Law of Evidence*)

God's Word is infallible- it is without error. But we also have God's Holy Spirit to convince us of His truth.[20] He has His ways of communicating to each one of us about who He is and the truth of His words to us.

In order for us to rejoice over the news of inheriting riches- the messenger must be reliable. The messenger who

---

[17] 2 Timothy 3:16
[18] Matthew 24:35; Mark 13:31; Luke 21:33
[19] Testimony of the Evangelists, by Simon Greenleaf
[20] Romans 8:16

brings us the news of our eternal inheritance is far more reliable than any human messenger. And we can absolutely rely on the messenger because the messenger is God Himself.

The second thing we mentioned about rejoicing over a message of a great inheritance was that we would need to believe that the inheritance is intended for us. It is. As we looked at earlier, if you have Jesus as your Lord and Savior, you have eternal life, and you will be going to Heaven for eternity. Those aren't just my words, those are God's words,[21] and God doesn't lie.[22]

What a Faith

This brings us to the essence of faith. What is true faith? Faith is believing God. God said it, we believe it, that settles it. Our faith stands and rests on God's Word. If God says something to you, should you believe it? Absolutely. God can't lie.[23] He will never tell a lie. It goes against His nature. He is good and Holy and pure. He is Light. There is nothing in God that is bad or evil. He will never change from being absolutely good and righteous.[24] When He says something, you can absolutely count on it.

As Christians, "we walk by faith, not by sight."[25] We can't see God. We can't see Heaven. Yet God and Heaven are real and eternal- they will last forever. And so will every word that God says. As Jesus said, "Heaven and earth shall pass away, but my words shall not pass away."[26] As the Apostle Paul said, "For the things which are seen are temporary, but the things which are not seen are eternal."[27] It could be said that our

---

[21] John 1:12; Romans 10:9-13; 1 John 5:11-13

[22] Numbers 23:19

[23] Malachi 3:6; Titus 1:2; James 1:17

[24] Hebrews 13:8

[25] 2 Corinthians 5:7

[26] Matthew 24:35, When Jesus used the word "Heaven" in this verse, He was referring to the sky.

[27] 2 Corinthians 4:18

faith, our trust, is in that which is truly real, even though we can't see it. Everything we can see with our eyes will only exist for a period of time, but our faith is in that which will last forever- the Living God and His Word.

There are times when we think God didn't mean what He said or do what He promised. We blame Him and are disappointed because we misunderstand what God has said. God always means what He says, and does what He says He will do. He may not do things the way we think He should, or when we think He should, but God always keeps His Word.

There is an interesting conversation that took place between Peter and Jesus. Jesus described how Peter would die. Peter quickly changed the subject and asked about another disciple, John,

> **Everything we can see with our eyes will only exist for a period of time, but our faith is in that which will last forever- the Living God and His Word.**

"'But Lord, what about this man?' Jesus said to him, 'If I will that he remain till I come, what is that to you? You follow Me.' Then this saying went out among the brethren that this disciple would not die. Yet Jesus did not say to him that he would not die, but, 'If I will that he remain till I come, what is that to you?'"[28] The disciples started thinking John would live until the second coming of Jesus, but that's not what Jesus said would happen. We see that at times, even the disciples who were with Jesus, misunderstood what He said because they didn't listen to Him carefully.

We should always listen carefully to what God says. He says what He means and means what He says. This is a wonderful truth. We can totally trust God. He will never let us down. As Moses said to Joshua, "He is the One who goes before you. He will be with you, He will not leave you nor forsake you; do not fear nor be dismayed."[29] And as the writer

---

[28] John 21:22-23
[29] Deuteronomy 31:8

of Hebrews tells us, "For He Himself has said, "I will never leave you nor forsake you."[30] God is absolutely faithful, so we can absolutely trust Him. And when Jesus said, "the one who comes to Me I will certainly not cast out,"[31] He meant it. The Good News is for you. You can rejoice over the news of your great inheritance because: Number one; The Messenger is absolutely reliable. And number two; The message is for you.

Lasting Joy

The third thing we need in order to rejoice over the message of our great inheritance, is to keep the inheritance in mind. If we get distracted by the cares of this life, or by anything, the promise of our inheritance will stop being a source of joy for us. You might think, "How can anyone forget that they are going to inherit $50 million?" Well, how can anyone forget a treasure that is worth infinitely more than $50 million- that God has forgiven them of all their sins, that He is with them, and that He has promised them eternity in Heaven? Unfortunately, the reality is that over time, we can easily forget it- or at least we can spend very little time thinking about it. So how can we abide in faith so that we might have continual joy?

> You might think, "How can anyone forget that they are going to inherit $50 million?" Well, how can anyone forget a treasure that is worth infinitely more than $50 million?

Abiding in Faith

One of the wonderful things about our faith is that it will grow as we continue to walk with God. As He shows Himself to be faithful to us, our faith will increase. But there are also things that we can do to strengthen our faith.

---

[30] Hebrews 13:5
[31] John 6:37 (NASB)

"Faith comes by hearing, and hearing by the word of God."[32] That's how our relationship with the Lord begins- with a message from God.

> One of the wonderful things about our faith is that it will grow as we continue to walk with God.

And that's how our faith grows. Jude says that you should be "building yourselves up on your most holy faith."[33] How do we do that?

You often hear people say things like, "Oh, how I wish I had greater faith." If your best friend tells you they are going to visit you this weekend, will you say, "Oh, how I wish I had greater faith to believe you! Help me to believe you!"? Probably not. Why not? Because you know your best friend and you trust them. The reason we don't trust God more is because we don't know Him well enough. How do we strengthen our faith in God? By getting to know Him better.

> If your best friend tells you they are going to visit you this weekend, will you say, "Oh, how I wish I had greater faith to believe you! Help me to believe you!"?

We get to know people better by spending time with them, and communicating with them. It's the same with God. The primary way to get to know and trust God more is through the Word of God. If you want to be a person of great faith; spend time every day reading the Bible and praying. Pray before you read, and as you read, seek to listen to what the Holy Spirit says to you. Don't be in a rush. The Lord will often speak to us with a "still, small voice"[34] as we read. The Bible is not just black (and red) ink on white paper. Jesus said, "The words that I speak to you are spirit, and they are life."[35] As we read the Bible with a listening heart, His words will "come alive" to us. If we just read the Bible without

---

[32] Romans 10:17

[33] Jude 1:20

[34] 1 Kings 19:12

[35] John 6:63

seeking to listen to the Holy Spirit as we read, we will miss out on a lot of what the Lord wants to say to us.

As you allow God to speak to you, and seek to listen to what He says, your faith will be strengthened, and your joy will increase. One of the tremendous benefits of spending time every day prayerfully reading the Bible is that you will be thinking a lot more about Heaven and the

> **If we read the Bible without seeking to listen to the Holy Spirit as we read, we will miss out on a lot of what the Lord wants to say to us.**

things of God. As we fix our minds on "eternal things,"[36] one result will be that we will keep our mind on the treasures of our inheritance, and the temporary things of this life will lose their ability to weigh us down.

One of the most well known passages in the Bible is Psalm One. It starts out by saying, "Blessed is the man who walks not in the counsel of the ungodly, nor stands in the path of sinners, nor sits in the seat of the scornful; but his delight is in the law of the LORD, and in His law he meditates day and night..."[37] The psalm then goes on to reveal to us the wonderful benefits of "meditating" in "His law" day and night (including prospering in whatever we do!). The first word of the psalm, "blessed," could also be translated as "happy." The word "law," could also be translated as "direction" or "instruction."

So the promise of God is that if we avoid the things mentioned in the beginning of the psalm, and we "meditate" (or think about, ponder) on God's Word, we will be happy. It sounds so easy, in fact it sounds too easy to be true, so we can easily spend huge amounts of time and energy trying to find joy in other ways. But our faith and our joy are totally dependent on us spending time taking in, praying about, and thinking about, God's Word. This truth is so simple and

---

[36] 2 Corinthians 4:8
[37] Psalm 1:1-2

powerful, and yet many of us run right past it. While the Lord is trying to lead us to "still waters,"[38] we are rushing off to the next activity, hobby or seminar- trying to find the best way to improve our lives.

Tonga

I owned a small, high-rise window cleaning business, and had been a Christian for about a year. I was cleaning a man's windows and he told me he was starting a Christian television station in the South Pacific island nation of Tonga. We talked about all the Mormons who live there who need to know the real Jesus. Since I had been involved in helping some Mormons come out of the deception of Mormonism, the man said, "Hey, why don't you pray about coming down to Tonga to help us start the television station?" To make a long story short, a few months later I was a missionary in Tonga.

I spent nine months in Tonga and about five months into my time there, I contracted a potentially fatal illness. I had a boil in my throat that felt like it was the size of a golf ball. I went to an American doctor who had a medical clinic on the island and he gave me some pain killers and antibiotics. My condition continued to deteriorate.

Since I was sick in bed, I thought I would take advantage of the opportunity to read the Bible. I was still new in my faith and hadn't read all the way through the Bible yet, so I decided to start at the beginning of the Bible and read it from cover to cover. As I read through a few of the Old Testament books that weren't all that exciting to me (like the book of Numbers), which talk about things like the number of people in different tribes, it occurred to me that parts of the Bible seemed to not feed my mind at all. I had to force myself to keep reading.

After having this illness for about two weeks, I was quite sick and in a lot of pain. In fact, I was in so much pain that I

---

[38] Psalm 23:2

hadn't been able to eat or sleep for three days. Then Sunday came. I was living with a wonderful man named Talakai, who is a retired pastor. As I lay in bed that Sunday morning, I asked Talakai, "Can you try to find the doctor at church today, to get more pain pills for me? I am in so much pain that I can't eat or sleep, even with the pain pills. It will be worse now that I've run out of them." He said, "Ok. But let's pray and ask God to heal you." We prayed for my healing. When we finished, Talakai said, "Let's praise the Lord." I looked up and as the first word of praise began to come out of my mouth, I was healed- instantly. It felt like the golf ball sized boil flew up through the ceiling. I was completely healed.

At the moment I was healed, I felt like God put it on my heart that part of the reason I was healed, was that my faith had been strengthened by reading the Bible. Even though I didn't feel anything from reading the Bible, and a lot of what I had been reading about the numbers of people in tribes, didn't seem to do anything for me mentally, my faith had been strengthened by reading God's Word. I wasn't "claiming" God's healing. I didn't know He was going to heal me. But I knew He could.

> **Even though I didn't feel anything from reading the Bible, my faith had been strengthened by reading God's Word.**

It's Not a Formula

There have been many times over the years that I have prayed for God's healing (for others, as well as for myself), and healing didn't happen. Does that mean my faith has decreased since I was healed in Tonga? No, reading the Bible and increased faith in God is not a formula for automatic healing. The Apostle Paul was a man of great faith, through whom God performed many miracles, including raising the dead,[39] and yet his great faith was not some kind of guarantee of healing.[40]

---

[39] Acts 20:7-10
[40] 1 Timothy 5:23; (Also, possibly 2 Corinthians 12:7-10)

In the same way, reading the Bible is not a guarantee of joy. The key to having the "joy of faith"[41] is found in our relationship with God. As we draw near to Him, He will draw near to us,[42] and as King David wrote, "in Your presence is fullness of joy."[43] Prayerfully reading God's Word, and meditating on it day and night, are powerful tools to help us draw closer to God, and to know Him better. How do we strengthen our faith? Not by striving after faith, but by resting on the Faithful One, and by spending time with Him in prayer and in His Word.

> How do we strengthen our faith? Not by striving after faith, but by resting on the Faithful One, and by spending time with Him in prayer and in His Word.

Positive Thanking

One of the results of developing a closer relationship with God, is that we will become more thankful. And thankfulness is one of the greatest ways to develop a closer relationship with God (which of course, will result in more joy in our lives). It's a win, win situation- the closer we get to God, the more thankful we are, and the more thankful we are, the closer we get to God.

As we see how faithful He is, and how He always keeps His promises, we should be thankful. As we reflect on God's goodness and thank and praise Him, our faith is strengthened. But thanking and praising God is something we need to choose to do. It's amazing how easy it is to neglect this very important part of our relationship with God.

In the first century, lepers were treated as social outcasts. They were banished from their family and neighbors. They weren't allowed to travel on the road and had to keep away from other people. If someone approached them, they had to

---

[41] Philippians 1:25
[42] James 4:8
[43] Psalm 16:11

warn them by shouting, "Unclean! Unclean!" so people would know to stay away from them. It was a dreaded disease and lepers lived a terrible life of isolation.

Jesus went into a village where there were ten lepers. "Then as He entered a certain village, there met Him ten men who were lepers, who stood afar off. 'Jesus, Master, have mercy on us!' So when He saw them, He said to them, 'Go, show yourselves to the priests.' And so it was that as they went, they were cleansed."[44]

When Jesus healed the ten men, only one of them returned to give Him thanks. We can easily marvel at the ingratitude of the nine lepers. Jesus freely healed them of a dreaded disease. How could they not thank Him? Yet, we can be just like these nine men. God has truly blessed us with unfathomable riches, is blessing us greatly every day, and will bless us tremendously for all of eternity, but we can easily go through our lives offering very little thanks to Him.

> God has truly blessed us with unfathomable riches, is blessing us greatly every day, and will bless us tremendously for all of eternity, yet we can easily go through our lives offering very little thanks to Him.

How much time do you spend thanking and praising God? More than five or ten seconds a day? We can wonder why we don't have a closer relationship with God, and yet we neglect one of the most important aspects of that relationship. The Apostle Paul tells us, "in everything give thanks; for this is the will of God in Christ Jesus for you."[45] Notice that He doesn't say to give thanks *for everything*, but to give thanks *in everything*. If my closest friend dies, I don't think God expects me to thank Him for that, but I can be thankful for what a blessing that friend has been in my life. There are

---

[44] Luke 17:13
[45] 1 Thessalonians 5:18

many things I can be thankful for no matter what situation I am in.

The psalmist writes, "Oh, give thanks to the LORD, for He is good! For His mercy endures forever."[46] No matter what we are going through, those are two things we can thank God for-His goodness and His mercy that lasts forever. Paul said, "And whatever you do in word or deed, do all in the name of the Lord Jesus, giving thanks to God the Father through Him."[47] So no matter what we do, we should be giving thanks as we do it. In fact, God tells us that thanksgiving is a key to overcoming anxiety and having peace- "Be anxious for nothing, but in everything by prayer and supplication, with thanksgiving, let your requests be made known to God; and the peace of God, which surpasses all understanding, will guard your hearts and minds through Christ Jesus."[48]

> "Oh, give thanks to the LORD, for He is good! For His mercy endures forever."
> - Psalm 107:1

Thankfulness is one of the keys to having a close relationship with God. As Psalm 100 says, "Enter into His gates with thanksgiving, and into His courts with praise. Be thankful to Him, and bless His name."[49] Under the old Covenant, the temple was where people went to meet with God, and God directed them to enter the gates of the temple with thanksgiving and praise. In the same way, for us today, praise and thanksgiving are a part of drawing near to God.

It's interesting that in describing the characteristics of ungodly and unrighteous people, Paul points out two things they did wrong: "they did not honor Him as God or give thanks."[50] A lack of thankfulness is a hallmark of the

---

[46] Psalm 107:1
[47] Colossians 3:17
[48] Philippians 4:6-7
[49] Psalm 100:4
[50] Romans 1:21 (NASB)

unrighteous, but thankfulness should be one of the hallmarks of a Christian.

If we want to be people who are filled with joy, we must be people who abide in faith- people who are spending time praying, reading God's Word, and praising and thanking God. As we do, we will meet the three requirements needed in order to rejoice over the news of our great inheritance- 1- We will realize that the messenger (God) is absolutely trustworthy; 2- We will see and be reminded of the fact that the message is indeed intended for us; and 3- We will think continually about our inheritance- and it will lead us to joy.

There is something else that is linked to our faith that is also a tremendous source of joy- our hope. As we will see in the next chapter, abiding in hope is also vital to living a life of joy. How can we abide in hope? Read on.

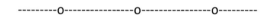

Heavenly Father, I believe You have a wonderful inheritance for me. You have truly blessed me, are blessing me, and will bless me, beyond all that I will ever deserve. Thank You. Thank You for being a God who is an absolutely reliable messenger. Thank You that the news of the great inheritance is for me. And thank You for giving me Your Holy Spirit, the Bible, circumstances, other people, and creation, to remind me of how faithful You are. Please help me to regularly spend time in prayer, praise, thanksgiving and reading the Bible. Please help me to continually think about my wonderful riches. Help me to abide in faith. In Jesus' name I pray, Amen.

7

Abiding in Hope

"But those who wait on the LORD shall renew their strength; they shall mount up with wings like eagles, they shall run and not be weary, they shall walk and not faint."

- Isaiah 40:31

High Hopes

When I was a little boy, I was skinny. I would get teased about it often. It didn't matter how much I ate. In fact, I ate a lot, but I was skinny for my entire childhood. I remember one night when one of my three (wonderful) sisters made spaghetti for dinner. It was delicious. I filled a plate from one edge to the other with a giant pile of spaghetti. Then I ate three more plates full- each of them piled high with spaghetti. People were amazed at how much I could eat, but I was still skinny.

My best friend's mother thought my mother must not be feeding me enough, so she took pity on me. Every day after school, I would go to my friend's house and his mother would make me pancakes- a lot of pancakes. Day after day, I would gorge myself on those wonderful pancakes. It was great. After a few weeks of this however, my friend's mother realized that, as she said, I must have a hollow leg, and she stopped making me pancakes.

Being skinny bothered me quite a bit- but I had hope. I wasn't very tall for my age and people kept telling me that one day, I was going to "shoot up" in height. I was excited. I couldn't wait to be tall. I had spent many years being skinny, but at least I had hope- I was going to be tall. Boy, was I going to be tall! Months went by, then years, and then more years. I kept waiting to shoot up. It didn't happen. Well, at least it didn't happen until what seemed like, many years had passed.

Hope Fulfilled

Then finally, I began to grow. My mother would draw lines with a pencil on one of our kitchen cabinets. We would write the date and my height next to the lines that were drawn. I was so excited to see that my hope was being fulfilled. All that waiting, and finally, the proof was on the wall- line after line of progress. As my three sisters grew slowly, there were the lines of skinny, little Strat. One after another, proving that yes indeed, I shot up!

My hope of becoming tall was a source of joy for me long before I started to grow much, even though the people that told me I would shoot up, didn't know for sure whether or not it would actually happen.

> **Hope is the forward focus of our faith.**

Our God is "the God of hope."[1] He is the source of our hope. But the hope He has for us is not like the hope of a 10 year old boy who wants to be tall. When the Bible speaks of the hope of the followers of Christ, it is talking about a sure hope, not a "hope so." The promise of Heaven is guaranteed.[2] Jesus said, "I go to prepare a place for you."[3] He created the entire universe,[4] so when He says, "I go to prepare a place for you," we can be assured it's going to be awesome.

Having hope is vital to us as Christians. Hope is the forward focus of our faith.

---

[1] Romans 15:13
[2] Ephesians 1:13-14
[3] John 14:2-3
[4] John 1:1-3; Colossians 1:16

Wanting and Waiting

There are two important elements of a Christian's hope: desire and expectation. We desire all of the wonderful things God has in store for us- being face to face with the God who is love, spending eternity in a place that's so awesome and wonderful that we can't even imagine it, being completely free from all temptation to sin, and having new and perfect bodies.

We desire to be united with other believers and family members who have lived throughout the ages. Everything about Heaven and our life after this one will be wonderful. It is all truly worthy of our desire.

Of course, many people desire things they will never get. Hundreds of millions of people enter sweepstakes, desiring to win millions of dollars. All of them, except for a very few, will be disappointed when they don't get what they desired. But Christians have more than just desire- the second element of our hope is expectation. Expectation is not wishful thinking. We are not just hoping to go to Heaven, like someone who enters a sweepstake is hoping to win. Ours is a sure hope- we are looking forward to the incredible blessings that await us, because God, "who cannot lie,"[5] has given us "exceedingly great and precious promises"[6] that are "more desirable than

> **There are two important elements of a Christian's hope: desire and expectation- wanting and waiting.**

gold."[7] We are "looking for the blessed hope and glorious appearing of our great God and Savior Jesus Christ."[8] We aren't just desiring Heaven- we are "looking for" it, waiting for it- expecting it!

The prophet Isaiah said, "But those who wait on the LORD shall renew their strength; they shall mount up with

---

[5] Titus 1:2
[6] 2 Peter 1:4
[7] Psalm 19:10; See also Matthew 6:19-21
[8] Titus 2:13

wings like eagles, they shall run and not be weary, they shall walk and not faint."[9] Those are amazing promises for us who wait on the Lord. As we "wait on Him"- looking forward to receiving what He has promised, we will have renewed strength to fly, run and walk through this life without becoming weary and fainting. There is a tremendous amount of strength that comes from the forward focus of our faith.

Most of us are familiar with Hebrews Chapter 11. It's been called the great "Hall of Faith." It's enlightening to read through the chapter and to look at all the passages that talk about looking to the future. Here are some of those passages (Notice the emphasis on looking to the future.)- "Now faith is the substance of things hoped for... the land of promise... he waited for the city... but having seen them afar off... But now they desire a better, that is, a heavenly country... concerning things to come... he looked to the reward... that they might obtain a better resurrection... the promise..." Over and over in the chapter, we see that future focus.

In fact, most of Hebrews 11 speaks about our future hope, and how God responds to those who have this hope- "These all died in faith, not having received the promises, but having seen them afar off were assured of them, embraced them and confessed that they were strangers and pilgrims on the earth. For those who say such things declare plainly that they seek a homeland. And truly if they had called to mind that country from which they had come out, they would have had opportunity to return. But now they desire a better, that is, a heavenly country. Therefore God is not ashamed to be called their God, for He has prepared a city for them."[10]

Why is God not ashamed to be called their God? Is it because they did some great work for Him? No, it's because "they desire a better, that is, a heavenly country."[11] They all, "not having received the promises, but having seen them afar

---

[9] Isaiah 40:31

[10] Hebrews 11:13-16

[11] Hebrews 11:16

off were assured of them, embraced them and confessed that they were strangers and pilgrims on the earth."[12] They were so Heavenly minded, so focused on God's promises about the future, that they saw themselves as "strangers and pilgrims on the earth." In modern terminology, we might describe that as a foreigner, an alien, or a camper. Do you see yourself as just a camper on this earth?

The Camping Trip

Having the mindset of a camper is critical to abiding in hope. It is so easy for us to be blinded to this truth. We tend to live as though life on earth is all there is. We stress and strain about all the things of this world. We focus on "the cares of this world, the deceitfulness of riches, and the desires for other things,"[13] and the riches of God's promises to us become something we only think about for a few fleeting moments every week as we sit or stand in church. We work so hard to hold on to our youth because we fear getting old. We campers should

> **Having the mindset of a camper is critical to abiding in hope.**

take care of our tents,[14] but how much time do we spend thinking about "the cares of this world" and how much time do we spend embracing, thinking about, and rejoicing over the promises of God? God help us to obey the command of Scripture to set our minds "on things above, not on things on the earth."[15] We're just camping here!

Paul tells us we don't lose heart because we "do not look at the things which are seen, but at the things which are not seen. For the things which are seen are temporary, but the things which are not seen are eternal."[16] The Word of God says if we live our lives fixing our minds on the things we see,

---

[12] Hebrews 11:13
[13] Mark 4:19
[14] 2 Corinthians 5:1
[15] Colossians 3:2
[16] 2 Corinthians 4:18

we will lose heart. This is a key to living a victorious Christian life. Nobody wants to lose heart- we want to be encouraged and to walk in joy. And in order to do that, it's crucial that we fix our minds on eternal things.

If you were to spend a morning walking along a beach at low tide, building sand castles at the water's edge, and then you were to walk by those sand castles a few hours later, hoping they would all still be there, you would be disappointed as you saw them one by one, or all at once, being reclaimed by the waves and the incoming tide. If you were to walk down the beach the next morning and the next, doing the same thing, each time building sand castles and hoping they would remain, you would eventually become discouraged. Why? Because of your unrealistic expectations. You might question the sanity of someone who would do such a thing, and yet how easy it is for us to be investing our energy and focus on building sand castles at the water's edge at low tide- those things that won't bring real joy, and won't last. We lose heart because we are constantly thinking about the temporal, and putting our hope in the things of this world.

> How easy it is for us to be investing our energy and focus on building sand castles at the water's edge at low tide.

Great News

I have some great news for you- you are going to die soon. Yes, that's great news. The best thing that could possibly happen to any Christian is that we would die. Why? (You should know the answer to this one.) Because we are going to Heaven! We're going to see the Lord face to face! That's awesome! As Paul said, "to die is gain"[17] and death for a Christian is "far better"[18] than living here on earth. (Of course, God has us here for good reasons so we should never seek to leave ahead of His time schedule.)

---

[17] Philippians 1:21
[18] Philippians 1:23

I saw a commercial in which an American sailor was speaking to a German soldier over the radio. The American sailor said, "Mayday! Mayday! We are sinking!" The German soldier (whose command of the English language wasn't very good) replied, "Vut are you sinking about?" We can so easily be worried about "sinking" in the worries of this world, when we should be "thinking" about Heaven and the life to come. We can be guilty of occasionally glancing at the future, when we should be fixated on it. Like a child who is expecting their father to return from the pet store any minute with a new puppy, we should be "eagerly waiting"[19] for our soon, short trip to Heaven.

An Anchored Hope

The writer of the book of Hebrews tells us, "This hope we have as an anchor of the soul, both sure and steadfast."[20] A number of years ago, I sat as a new believer in a chair in my mother's kitchen. I was discussing my new found faith in Christ with one of my (wonderful) older sisters and a friend of my mother's, who was a retired Biology professor. As we talked, the subject of evolution was brought up. As a new Christian, I had very little knowledge of the evidence against the idea of all life evolving by random chance from a rock, and both my sister and the professor had been fed a steady stream of the evolutionary religion in their grade school, high school and university educations, so I was outgunned.

As they mentioned point after point they thought supported the fairy tale of their evolutionary religion, I couldn't respond with any scientific facts that supported the truth of God's amazing design in His creation of life. It was two against one, and they had "the facts." As they barraged me with "evidence," I had an amazing experience. I couldn't answer their questions and I couldn't explain how I knew they were wrong, but I knew that I knew they were wrong and that

---

[19] Romans 8:23
[20] Hebrews 6:19

I had the truth. It felt like there was an anchor with a line going from me downward. I could get knocked a bit to one side or the other, but I was anchored in the truth. They couldn't take my hope away from me. I knew it was the truth. Months later, when I first read Hebrews 6:19, where Paul says, "This hope we have as an anchor of the soul, both sure and steadfast,"[21] I was amazed. That's exactly what it felt like- an anchor of my soul, "both sure and steadfast." Even though the storms of life will come, and we may get knocked around, our hope is like an anchor, a sure and steadfast anchor, that helps us to weather the storms- whenever they come and however fierce they may be.

A Purifying Hope

Another wonderful thing about our hope is that it has a purifying effect on us. As the Apostle John wrote, "Beloved, now we are children of God; and it has not yet been revealed what we shall be, but we know that when He is revealed, we shall be like Him, for we shall see Him as He is."[22] When we

> "This hope we have as an anchor of the soul, both sure and steadfast."
> - Hebrews 6:19

see the Lord face to face, we will be changed.[23] The instant we see Him, we will be radically different. Just as turning a light on in a dark room instantly affects things in the room, when we see the Lord face to face, the radiance of His glory will instantly affect us- we will be changed. We really can't imagine exactly what that will be like, but if you were standing in a cold, dark room long enough to be feeling very cold, and then you were instantly transported to be standing in front of a warm fire, there would be an immediate change. You would be affected by the light, the warmth and the glow of the fire. Of course, the example of a warm fire falls far short. Any earthly comparison we could

---

[21] Hebrews 6:19

[22] 1 John 3:2

[23] 1 Corinthians 15:51

think of is almost ridiculous compared to the change we will experience by being in the presence of the Lord- the Almighty, glorious God.

Right after saying we will be changed by being in His presence and seeing Him as He is, John says, "And everyone who has this hope in Him purifies himself, just as He is pure."[24] In other words, as we hope in Christ, and look forward to His appearing and to being with Him in Heaven, we will become more pure- more like Him. Thinking about the Lord and Heaven continually, will change us. Have you ever noticed how people become like what they fix their hearts and minds on (their gods)? The psalmist writes, "The idols of the nations are but silver and gold, the work of man's hands. They have mouths, but they do not speak; they have eyes, but they do not see; they have ears, but they do not hear, nor is there any breath at all in their mouths. Those who make them will be like them, yes, everyone who trusts in them."[25] People who live for the things of this world become like the things of this world. People who love money, for example, become cold and unfeeling- just like money. People who live for the Lord and Heavenly things, who fix their minds on things above, will become more like them- they will be purified and will become better people. As Paul says, "But we all, with unveiled face, beholding as in a mirror the glory of the Lord, are being transformed into the same image from glory to glory."[26] I want to be a better person, and by hoping in Him, praying to Him, and by thinking about Him and His words to me- I will be transformed.

> "But we all... beholding as in a mirror the glory of the Lord, are being transformed into the same image from glory to glory." - 2 Corinthians 3:18

---

[24] 1 John 3:3

[25] Psalm 135:15-18 (NASB)

[26] 2 Corinthians 3:18

Hope Under Attack

The Apostle Peter warned us "that scoffers will come in the last days, walking according to their own lusts, and saying, 'Where is the promise of His coming?'"[27] Notice that Peter predicted that the attacks of the scoffers against Christians would be against our hope- the promise of the coming of the Lord. Peter goes on to say, "The Lord is not slack concerning His promise, as some count slackness, but is longsuffering toward us, not willing that any should perish but that all should come to repentance."[28] Jesus will fulfill His promise to come back and take us to Heaven, but God is longsuffering, giving people time to repent (turn away from sin, and put their faith in Christ). Then Peter says, "But the day of the Lord will come as a thief in the night, in which the heavens will pass away with a great noise, and the elements will melt with fervent heat; both the earth and the works that are in it will be burned up."[29]

"It's All Going to Burn"

The earth and its atmosphere, everything we can see, "the heavens and the earth," will be burned up in a few moments of time. All those things people worked so hard to build, all those fortunes people worked so hard to gain, all those treasures people worked so hard to store up on earth- will be destroyed in an instant. God brought judgment on the earth in Noah's day- He flooded it with water. God is going to judge the earth again, but this time it will be with fire. It will give a whole new meaning to the term "global warming." When I first became a Christian, there was a saying that was popular among Christians I knew- "It's all going to burn!" It was an encouragement for us not to hold things too tightly, knowing

---

[27] 2 Peter 3:3-4
[28] 2 Peter 3:9
[29] 2 Peter 3:10

that everything we see around us is temporary, and one day, it will all burn up.

As you read these verses in Second Peter, there are a couple of things repeated over and over. Notice the repetition of the fact that the earth and it's atmosphere will be destroyed by fire- "But the heavens and the earth... are reserved for fire... will melt with fervent heat... will be burned up... will be dissolved... will be dissolved, being on fire... will melt with fervent heat."[30] It's quite repetitive. Obviously, God really wants us to get the point- it's all going to burn!

The second thing that's repeated in this passage is regarding our response to this reality. It has to do with our focus- what we think about. He says we should be "...*looking for*... the coming of the day of God... we... *look for* new heavens and a new earth... *looking forward* to these things..."[31] Just as God repeats over and over that judgment is coming and that the earth will be destroyed by fire, He also repeats over and over that we should be looking forward- we must persevere in hope.

I'm Going to Heaven!

Years ago, I heard a story about an elderly pastor. He had been the pastor of a small congregation for many years. For some reason, the church leaders had decided to replace him with another pastor. The leaders of the church met with the pastor and gave him the news. Since they had known him for many years, he was a friend of theirs and they had concern for his welfare. He had a smile on his face after they told him they were firing him. One of the church leaders asked, "What are you going to do?" He replied, "I'm going to Heaven!" The leader said, "We know that but you are losing your income and you won't have money to live on." The pastor said, "I'm going to Heaven!" One after another, the leaders questioned him about his future welfare. And to question after question,

---

[30] 2 Peter 3:7, 10-12
[31] 2 Peter 3:12-14

the pastor replied, "I'm going to Heaven!" He didn't know what would happen in the near future. He didn't know how he would be provided for financially. But he knew he was going to Heaven and that's all that really mattered. Like this elderly pastor, no matter what we endure in this life, we can always say, "I'm going to Heaven!"

The words of Romans 15:13- "May the God of hope fill you with all joy and peace in believing, so that by the power of the Holy Spirit you may abound in hope," had come to life for this pastor. And they have come alive for so many Dalit Christians in India and Nepal, and in the lives of millions of our brothers and sisters living in Muslim, Hindu, Buddhist and Communist countries around the world, where Christians' lives are in danger daily from the enemies of the Cross. Their forward focus, their hope, is an anchor of their souls. At the time of the writing of this book, there are numerous reports of Christian children in the Middle East having their heads chopped off by radical Muslims because they won't deny their faith. How can they be willing to die rather than deny the Lord? Their hope is an anchor, "sure and steadfast."

The Hope of Righteousness

Every human being who has ever lived has struggled with sin. While the natural human tendency is to give in to sin, it is a monster that cannot be tamed. Once it is allowed in, it takes over. Of course, there is an escape from the power of sin, and it's found only in Jesus. When we receive Jesus as our Lord and Savior, we are delivered from the penalty of sin (eternal separation from God in Hell), and the power of sin- we have the Holy Spirit to help us resist the temptation to sin. How wonderful it is that we have the Helper. As long as we are in these fleshly bodies however, we still struggle with sin. Every day, we can thank the Lord for His mercy, and every day we can ask for His help in resisting sin. Jesus taught us to pray,

"And do not lead us into temptation, but deliver us from the evil one."[32]

It's wonderful that He is our "refuge and strength, a very present help in trouble."[33] But (as we looked at in Chapter 2), one day soon, our struggle with sin will end completely. Part of our sure hope is the promise of God's complete deliverance from sin. We have "the hope of righteousness."[34] When we are changed into His likeness and brought to Heaven, we will be conformed to the likeness of Christ to such a degree that we will not be tempted by sin ever again- we will be righteous. When we are in Heaven, we won't be battling within ourselves to remain faithful to Christ. It will be "automatic." We will no longer live by faith, we will live by sight. We will see Him face to face, and never again be tempted to stray. Oh, what a sweet victory that will be! You and I will never be tempted again- ever! We will never again feel the pull of the things of this world. We will never again groan within ourselves, wishing to be set free from this body of sin and death.[35] We will never again feel the guilt of our conscience telling us we have sinned. We will truly have rest. What a joy that will be, and what a joy we can have now, knowing that our righteousness is coming soon- that "when He is revealed, we shall be like Him."[36] Oh, how glorious! It's no wonder the Apostle Paul tells us we should be "rejoicing in hope."[37]

Here Come the Rewards!

When you think of people in Heaven receiving rewards for things they've done on this earth, do you think of people like the Apostles- Paul and Peter? What about you? Do you picture yourself standing before the Judgment seat of Christ,

---

[32] Luke 11:4
[33] Psalm 46:1
[34] Galatians 5:5
[35] Romans 8:23
[36] 1 John 3:2
[37] Romans 12:12

getting a reward? Maybe you don't think you've been holy enough in this life to earn a reward from God. Well, guess what? Jesus said, "whoever gives one of these little ones only a cup of cold water in the name of a disciple, assuredly, I say to you, he shall by no means lose his reward."[38] You have probably done even more for Jesus than to give someone a cup of cold water. Have you served the Lord? Have you given to His people? Have you tried to bless someone for the sake of Jesus? If you have, think of all the rewards you have coming! You will be blessed indeed. In fact, Jesus said at times we are serving Him without even knowing it.[39] We will receive rewards for every single thing we have ever done for Him. I can't wait.

As Christians, we will all stand before Jesus at the "Bema," or "the judgment seat" of Christ. This is the place where the Lord will give rewards to Christians.[40] During the Olympic Games of Paul's day, wreaths were given out as rewards to those who had won a race. Paul spoke of the Bema of Christ, saying that "Do you not know that those

> Jesus said, "whoever gives one of these little ones only a cup of cold water in the name of a disciple, assuredly, I say to you, he shall by no means lose his reward."

who run in a race all run, but one receives the prize? Run in such a way that you may obtain it... Now they do it to obtain a perishable crown, but we for an imperishable crown."[41] We don't run the Christian race hoping to receive a "perishable crown," a wreath made of leaves, we run to receive an imperishable crown, a reward that will last forever. In fact, Jesus said, "Do not store up for yourselves treasures on earth, where moth and rust destroy, and where thieves break in and

---

[38] Matthew 10:42

[39] Matthew 25:34-40

[40] This is not the Great White Throne of Judgment- the place where punishment is given out to unbelievers.

[41] 1 Corinthians 9:24-25

steal. But store up for yourselves treasures in heaven, where neither moth nor rust destroys, and where thieves do not break in or steal."[42] We can live our lives storing up treasures in Heaven- treasures worth looking forward to.

More Than a Day's Pay

Jesus also said, "He who receives a prophet in the name of a prophet shall receive a prophet's reward. And he who receives a righteous man in the name of a righteous man shall receive a righteous man's reward."[43] In other words, we will be given rewards that are far more than what we've earned. All we have to do is to receive a prophet or a righteous person for the sake of Jesus, and we will receive the same reward as a prophet or a righteous person. That's amazing. It will be a lot better than working for one minute to receive a year's pay. Our God is a blessing God.

I once heard a comedian say that when people get to Heaven, there will be a big pile of all the pens, car keys and other things we had lost on earth. Nope. We won't receive any of our lost pens or car keys in Heaven; we will receive treasures that are worth far more than anything on this earth. We are going to Heaven! This truth should radically and continually impact our lives. And we should live this life looking forward to receiving those incredible rewards from the God who loves to give us wonderful things that we don't deserve, just because He loves us. We look forward in hope- in desire and expectation, wanting and waiting for the wonderful things God has in store for us. And it brings us joy- the joy that comes from good news from a country we have not yet visited, but have seen from a distance, a country that cannot be adequately described by words- a country that is wonderful beyond our wildest dreams, hopes or imagination. We have a hope that causes us to rejoice and keeps us going even when everything around us is failing, because it is a sure hope, it is a

---

[42] Matthew 6:19-20 (NASB)
[43] Matthew 10:41

wonderful hope and it is a hope worth rejoicing in.[44] And as we will see in the next chapter, there is something even greater than hope.

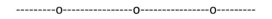

Heavenly Father, Thank You for giving me a sure hope. Thank You for being the God who is faithful to fulfill all Your promises. Help me to take my eyes off of the sand castles of this world- I know it's all going to burn. I desire what You have in store for me, and I expect to receive it because You are a God who cannot lie. Thank You that my hope is an anchor for my soul, and that as I fix my mind on Jesus and Heaven, I will become more like You. Thank You that my hope causes me to rejoice and I can always rejoice, knowing that I am going to Heaven and that one day my struggle against sin will end completely- You will make me perfectly righteous. Thank You for Your promises about my future rewards- rewards that I know I really don't deserve. Thank You for loving me so much. Help me to abide and rejoice in hope. In Jesus' name I pray, Amen.

---

[44] Romans 12:12

8

Abiding in Love

**"And now abide faith, hope, love, these three;
but the greatest of these is love."**
- 1 Corinthians 13:13

Have you ever noticed how two people facing the same difficulty can approach it with radically different viewpoints? To one person the trial is horrible. It's a reason to become really upset and discouraged. To another person the same trial looks like a speed bump. They may not immediately know how they are going to get through it, but they know they will. They have hope, optimism and even joy. "Don't they realize how serious their situation is?" You would think they must live a totally blessed life. What makes them so different?

Doreen and I were blessed by being able to go to Israel a few years ago. I had hoped to make a trip there at least once in my life and since we got a great deal on the trip and believing the Lord was leading us to go, we went. Getting to walk where Jesus walked was truly a life enriching experience and we were amazed by the number of archeological sites that validate the truth of the Bible. And just as we had heard it would, experiencing Israel first hand, made the Bible go from black and white, to color. It was wonderful. We had been there for just a few days when the thought hit me, "I can't wait to come back!" It was a life changing trip and we now recommend it to anyone who has any interest whatsoever in going there. One of the highlights of the trip was going out on the Sea of Galilee at sunset. As the setting sun reflected on the glassy water and the small ripples lapped against the boat, I couldn't help but think that Jesus and the disciples probably experienced the exact same thing when they were in a boat on that Sea.

The Sea of Galilee

The Sea of Galilee is actually a fresh water lake fed by the Jordan River. It teams with life and is Israel's largest and most important source of drinking water. For thousands of years, the Sea of Galilee has been a rich source of fish. The first-century historian Josephus wrote about the Sea of Galilee, saying, "One may call this place the ambition of nature." He reported a thriving fishing industry, with 230 boats fishing in the lake. While the number of fish has declined in recent years, in 2005, there were 500 tons of fish caught in the Sea of Galilee.

There is another Sea in Israel that is also fed by the Jordan River but it's very different from the Sea of Galilee. It's called the Dead Sea. There are no fish in the Dead Sea. As we drove up to the Dead Sea, we couldn't help but notice that there are no plants growing on its banks. Nobody can drink the water from the Dead Sea. There are good reasons why people call it the Dead Sea. Both seas are fed by the Jordan River. Why does one team with life while the other is almost completely dead? Simply put, the Dead Sea has no rivers flowing out of it. It is not a source of life-giving water. It receives but does not give.

It's the same for us as people. Why does one person face a difficulty with hope and joy, while another faces the same difficulty with hopelessness and despair? It may have a lot to do with the fact that one person may live life receiving and giving, while the other person lives life just seeking to receive.

The Joy of Giving and Serving

A couple of months after receiving the Lord, I had an opportunity to bless an elderly pastor. He was running a hunger mission on O'ahu where he would grow tropical plants and bring people from other countries and teach them about nutrition and tropical agriculture. I was a high-rise window cleaner so I didn't have a problem with heights. The pastor needed some vines cut that were hanging down from a tall tree and blocking a driveway. I set up my 36 foot ladder and as I got up to the top of the ladder to snip the vines, I felt a tremendous sense of joy. It was totally unexpected. I was flooded with joy. Wow! I was just cutting a few vines. What could explain that joy? I believe it was the Holy Spirit filling me with joy as I served the Lord. God was showing me the joy of serving others.

Obviously, we are not going to feel waves of joy every time we choose to put others first and serve the Lord, but Jesus meant it when He said, "whoever desires to save his life will lose it, but whoever loses his life for My sake will find it."[1]

You can't out give God. Notice that when Jesus described what will happen when we give, the result of the giving was far more than what was given- "Give, and it will be given to you. They will pour into your lap a good measure- pressed down, shaken together, and running over. For by your standard of measure it will be measured to you in return."[2] We will be tremendously blessed as we try to bless others. This is such a basic and simple fact of Christianity and yet we can live our whole Christian life skating on the edge of this truth.

Paul tells us that "the fruit of the Spirit is love, joy, peace, longsuffering, kindness, goodness, faithfulness, gentleness, self-control."[3] Notice that verse doesn't say "the fruits of the Spirit." The word "fruit" is singular. You could say there is only one real fruit of the Spirit- love. The rest of the words in that verse define that love. As the late pastor Chuck Smith said, "Joy is love's consciousness. (Have) you ever seen a

---

[1] Matthew 16:25
[2] Luke 6:38 (NASB)
[3] Galatians 5:22-23

person in love and all of the joy that they have?"[4] Jesus said, "abide in My love... that My joy may remain in you, and that your joy may be full."[5] Jesus said it best- if we are people who are filled with God's love, we will be people who are filled with His joy.

Paul tells us, "And now abide faith, hope, love, these three; but the greatest of these is love."[6] Why is love greater than faith and hope? Because love encompasses faith and hope. As we are told in 1 Corinthians Chapter 13, love believes all things and hopes all things.[7] The greatest thing you can possess is love.

Abundant Life

If we want to live the life that Jesus came to give us- the "abundant life,"[8] a life filled with joy and fruitfulness- we need to give our lives to Jesus. He said the great commandment is to "love the LORD your God with all your heart, with all your soul, and with all your mind,"[9] and the second great commandment is like the first one, "You shall love your neighbor as yourself."[10] When I was in India, I met Sanjay,[11] a missionary who serves in Northern India. I asked him if he had ever been persecuted. He said he had been beaten many times. He told me about several different occasions. One time he and a team of Indian missionaries were passing out Gospel tracts at train stations. They would pass out tracts to a massive crowd at one station

> **Jesus said it best- if we are people who are filled with God's love, we will be people who are filled with His joy.**

---

[4] Chuck Smith, C2000 Series on Galatians 5-6
[5] John 15:9, 11
[6] 1 Corinthians 13:13
[7] 1 Corinthians 13:7
[8] John 10:10
[9] Matthew 22:37
[10] Matthew 22:38
[11] Not his real name. I changed it for security purposes.

and then get on the train and ride to the next station where they would again find thousands of people who were unreached with the Gospel. At one of the stations, after passing out tracts, as he climbed up the stairs onto the train, a huge man came up behind him and yanked him off the train. He started beating Sanjay and Sanjay fell to the ground.

Like a Melon

The huge man kept beating and kicking Sanjay for quite some time, and then he ran off into the crowd. Sanjay rose to his feet and as soon as he could regain his balance, he took off running as well- but not to get away. He ran after his attacker- in order to give him a Gospel tract! Sanjay said his head was swollen "like a melon" for two months. As he told me this story, his eyes welled up with tears of joy as he said, "I am so privileged to be beaten for Jesus' sake. I am so blessed that He counted me worthy to suffer for Him." I was amazed not only by Sanjay's willingness to give his life and to suffer for the Lord, but also by the tears of joy that he shed as he recounted his experiences to me.

Sanjay is a man who is filled with joy. He gets it- he understands what Jesus meant when He said "whoever desires to save his life will lose it, but whoever loses his life for My sake will find it."[12] As Sanjay is giving his life for Jesus' sake, God is filling Sanjay with His joy. Does this mean that in order to have fullness of joy, you need to tell people about Jesus until you finally find some big guy who will beat and kick you until your head swells up like a melon? No. But we see in Sanjay, a person who says, "Not my will, Lord, but Yours be done," a person who says, "I am willing to follow You, Jesus. I love you and I am willing to do whatever You want me to do. I know Your plans are good and Your rewards are great." Sanjay is living a surrendered life. He wants to live

---

[12] Matthew 16:25

His life to please God, and he is willing to live for God and for heavenly rewards by loving his neighbors here on this earth.

As we surrender our lives to the Lord, God will probably not call most of us to go to a foreign mission field where Christians are beaten and killed for Christ. (If He does, that's great too- Heaven is a "far better"[13] place than the earth, and the sooner we get there, the sooner we'll be in the absolute fullness of joy in His presence.) But each one of us can choose to be like the Sea of Galilee, which pours out blessings, or we can be like the Dead Sea, which receives abundantly, but doesn't pour out any blessings. We can say, "Lord, I love you. I want to do Your will. I want to be surrendered to You. I want to live an 'abundant life.'[14] Help me to lay down my life for You, as You laid down Your life for me. What do you want me to do?"

Cool Water

God may lead you to give someone a cool glass of water. He may lead you to start reaching out to your neighbors with His love and truth. He may lead you to start teaching Sunday school at your church. He may lead you to serve Him in an inner city mission. He may (and probably will) lead you to get serious about your prayer life (if you aren't already). God has specific things He wants you to do. As Paul tells us, "we are His workmanship, created in Christ Jesus for good works, which God prepared beforehand that we should walk in them."[15] Do you want to miss out on the works that God has prepared especially for you? He has gifted you in ways you may not even know about, and He, the Creator of the universe, wants to use you to bless others for His sake. He will empower you and gift you and use you to bless others for His glory, and then when you get to Heaven, He will reward you

---

[13] Philippians 1:23
[14] John 10:10
[15] Ephesians 2:10

openly.[16] You will be honored by God Himself, in front of the angels in Heaven. And as you enter Heaven, God will say to you, "Well done, good and faithful servant; you were faithful over a few things, I will make you ruler over many things. Enter into the joy of your lord."[17]

As we choose to give our lives to please the Lord, and choose to love others for His sake, we will truly find our lives. The degree to which we give our life to Christ, is the degree to which we will have an abundant life. You can't go through this Christian life thinking, "Well, I'm not really into the 'give my life away' thing," and think you will have a life of joy and peace. "'There is no peace for the wicked,' says the LORD."[18] And whether you are an unbeliever living in total rebellion against God, or a Christian who is resisting the Lordship of Christ, you will not have peace until you are willing to draw a line in the sand and say, "Lord, I am on Your side. I surrender to You." Paul tells us that Jesus "died for all, so that they who live might no longer live for themselves, but for Him who died and rose again on their behalf."[19]

How High?

An amazing thing about this whole process is that as we fix our eyes on Jesus and on Heaven, surrender will be easy. Jesus said, "My yoke is easy and My burden is light."[20] Giving our lives to Jesus is easy if it's a response to His love and mercy. As Paul says, "I beseech you therefore, brethren, by the mercies of God, that you present your bodies a living sacrifice, holy, acceptable to God, which is your reasonable service."[21] Notice that the verse starts out with "I beseech you therefore, brethren, by the mercies of God." This is critical. Paul doesn't

---

[16] Matthew 6:4
[17] Matthew 25:21
[18] Isaiah 48:22
[19] 2 Corinthians 5:15 (NASB)
[20] Matthew 11:30
[21] Romans 12:1

say, "You'd better give your life to God!" No, he says, "by the mercies of God... present your bodies a living sacrifice... which is your reasonable service." In other words, "Seeing how incredibly merciful God is to you, I urge you to continually surrender your life to Him. It's the reasonable thing to do."

As the Apostle John said, "We love Him because He first loved us."[22] It could be said that this verse is the key to living the Christian life. It's the key to joy and peace, it's the key to victory over sin, it's the key to hope and it's the key to abiding in Christ- we love Him because He first loved us. Have you ever spent time praying about that verse? I encourage you to take some time to do that. Think about it. Talk to God about it. Listen to what He will say to you through it. It could change your life.

> An amazing thing about this whole process is that as we fix our eyes on Jesus and on Heaven, surrender will be easy.

God, the Creator of the universe, took on human flesh and came and suffered and died on a cross for you. Doesn't it make sense that you would be willing to be a living sacrifice for Him? Not out of guilt, but as a response to His amazing love, grace and mercy. He's taking us to Heaven as a free gift. He knows all things. He loves us and His plans are good. If He says "Jump," we want to say, "How high, Lord?" If He says to love our neighbors, we want to love our neighbors- even if they seem difficult to love or they persecute us.

> "We love Him because He first loved us." It could be said that this verse is the key to living the Christian life. It's the key to joy and peace, it's the key to victory over sin, it's the key to hope and it's the key to abiding in Christ.

God is worthy of us giving our short, little lives to Him. Or do we think more highly of ourselves than that? Do we say,

---

[22] 1 John 4:19

"What do you mean, 'little lives?' I have a big, important life." Well, "Behold, the nations are like a drop from a bucket, and are regarded as a speck of dust on the scales... All the nations are as nothing before Him, they are regarded by Him as less than nothing."[23] The next time you feel important and think you are something, you might want to read Job, Chapters 38 and 39. As He says, "Where were you when I laid the foundations of the earth? Tell Me, if you have understanding. Who determined its measurements? Surely you know! Or who stretched the line upon it? To what were its foundations fastened? Or who laid its cornerstone, when the morning stars sang together, and all the sons of God shouted for joy?"

"Or who shut in the sea with doors, when it burst forth and issued from the womb; when I made the clouds its garment, and thick darkness its swaddling band; when I fixed My limit for it, and set bars and doors; when I said, 'This far you may come, but no farther, and here your proud waves must stop!' Have you commanded the morning since your days began, and caused the dawn to know its place?"[24] God is Almighty, and truly, we are "less than nothing."[25] King David wrote, "When I consider Your heavens, the work of Your fingers, the moon and the stars, which You have ordained, what is man that You are mindful of him?"[26] We are not worthy to serve Him, but He loves us so much that He gives us the wonderful opportunity to serve Him and even to please Him. It's amazing.

The Joy of Surrender

Joy is not found by seeking hard after joy. Joy is found by seeking hard after God. As Malcolm Muggeridge, the late journalist and author said "I can say that I never knew what joy was like until I gave up pursuing happiness, or cared to

---

[23] Isaiah 40:15,17
[24] Job 38:4-12
[25] Isaiah 40:17
[26] Psalm 8:3-4

live until I chose to die." Jesus' words, "whoever desires to save his life will lose it, but whoever loses his life for My sake will find it,"[27] are not words of misery and death- they are words of absolute fullness of life and joy. It's only in losing our lives that we truly find them- and with our lives, we find a rich, deep, indescribable joy.

The Grand Exchange

As we choose to give our lives to Jesus, we exchange our lives for His. We give Him our burdens, our sin, our pain and our grief. He gives us a life of fruitfulness and joy that we could never dream of living on our own. We experience peace and fulfillment that we never could have found otherwise. And we realize that the trade is definitely worth making. I'll gladly give up my stress and

> Jesus' words, "whoever desires to save his life will lose it, but whoever loses his life for My sake will find it," are not words of misery and death- they are words of absolute fullness of life and joy.

struggling and defeat in order to experience His joy and fruitfulness. You might ask, "So what does it look like? What do I have to do? Exactly what do I have to give up?" Good questions. It looks different for you than it does for me. We can't necessarily tell who around us is living a surrendered life. And it is not our job to judge them. We should focus on what the Lord is leading us to do. When Jesus was telling Peter about how he was going to die, Peter, speaking of John, said, "What about this man?"[28] Jesus answered, "If I will that he remain till I come, what is that to you? You follow Me."[29] That's the call for every one of us- "You follow Me."

I wish I could say, "Yup. I've got the 'surrender to God' thing wired." I wish I could say that I am a 100% totally surrendered, moment by moment living sacrifice for God, but

---

[27] Matthew 16:25
[28] John 12:21
[29] John 21:22

I can't and I'm not. Ask anyone who knows me well, I fall far short. Every one of us is a work in progress. Nobody has arrived. Even the great Apostle Paul said, "Not that I have already attained, or am already perfected; but I press on, that I may lay hold of that for which Christ Jesus has also laid hold of me."[30] Paul pressed on, wanting to know the Lord and His love more fully so that he would be more completely given over to God. And that's where we are as well- not having arrived, but saying, "God, please make me willing to be willing to do Your will." And as we say that, God sees our hearts, He is pleased, and He rejoices.

You might think, "I fall so far short. I could never 'please God.'" Can you pray for someone? Can you give someone a cold drink of water? Can you believe God's Word? All of these things please God. He is blessed by every single thing we do for Him and by every desire we have to please Him. You might say, "But you don't know how many times I've walked away from God and how far I've gone. There's no way He could love me." Jesus came to seek and save the lost.[31] As Paul says, "This is a faithful saying and worthy of all acceptance, that Christ Jesus came into the world to save sinners, of whom I am chief."[32] He came to save sinners, like Paul, and you and me. He is not only the God of second chances- He is the God of 5,372nd chances. As Paul says, "Who is he who condemns? It is Christ who died, and furthermore is also risen, who is even at the right hand of God, who also makes intercession for us. Who shall separate us from the love of Christ?"[33] Jesus loves you, and He wants to bless you and use you.

---

[30] Philippians 3:12
[31] Luke 19:10
[32] 1 Timothy 1:15
[33] Romans 8:34-35

Learning from Love

At the time I am writing this book, I have been a Christian for 25 years. It's not a real long time, and I am not a great Christian. I'm just a regular guy, but if someone were to ask me what one thing I have learned more than any other about God, I would have to say, "God loves me." My realization that God loves me was a big part of why I became a Christian. I was amazed at this truth 25 years ago, and I am still amazed at it now. Before I received the Lord, my pride had caused me to think I was a pretty good person. Soon after receiving Jesus, I started to realize what a sinner I was. Now, 25 years later, I can't believe what a sinner I am, and God still says, "I love you." It's amazing.

And God knows how far short I'll fall tomorrow, and the next day, and the next, and yet He continues to love me. A part of me just can't get over it. How could He love me? Every day of my life I have selfish thoughts that I need to take "captive to the obedience of Christ."[34] Every day I sin and fall short- but God loves me anyway. Every person on earth falls short every day.[35] King David asked, "What is man that You are mindful of him?" But the question that demands to be asked is "Who are You God, that You are mindful of man?" The reason God loves us has to do with His nature- what's in Him; not our nature and what's in us. He loves us because of who He is. Knowing this truth will change our lives. Your life is not about measuring up to God's standards of absolute perfection so He will love you- your life is about loving Him and loving your neighbors, because He

> Soon after receiving Jesus, I started to realize what a sinner I was. Now, 25 years later, I can't believe what a sinner I am, and God still says, "I love you." It's amazing.

---

[34] 2 Corinthians 10:5
[35] Romans 3:23; 1 John 1:8

loved you first. As King Solomon said, "I am my beloved's, and my beloved is mine."[36]

God of the Knuckleheads

The sooner we grab hold of this truth, the better. God is love. He is the God who loves the unlovable- the knuckleheads. In case you hadn't noticed- that's us. The sooner we start to live our lives as a response to His love, rather than by trying to earn His love, the sooner we will start to walk in the abundant life- the life of joy and fruitfulness. The more you realize how great God's love for you is, the more you will love God. He is the initiator, we are the responders. He is the Groom, we are the bride. As we draw near to God with our hearts, He will draw near to us.[37] If we want to walk closely with God, it starts with our hearts. When Jesus gave us the great commandment, saying, "You shall love the LORD your God with all your heart, with all your soul, and with all your mind,"[38] notice that He started with the heart. That's the key- we should love God with all our hearts as a response to who He is and what He's done (and what He will do). As Paul says, "In view of God's mercy, present yourselves to God as a living sacrifice."

The Main Thing

In the Christian life, love is central. It is critical that we heed Paul's words and keep His mercy in view. Continually realizing God's love for us will result in us wanting to live lives that honor and glorify God. Our reasonable response to His love and mercy is that we want to pour out our lives in loving Him and loving others. In the same way that the Sea of Galilee needs to receive life giving water, and also pour out life giving water, and it results in health for the Sea of Galilee, so we need to receive the Living Water from God, and we need to

---

[36] Solomon 6:3
[37] James 4:8
[38] Matthew 22:37

pour it out as well. This will result in a life that pleases God, fruit that will last for eternity, and it will result in the abundant joy of God being in our lives. Giving people are joyful people, if their motivation comes from the fact that they know that God first loved them.

And as we will see in the next chapter, keeping God's love in mind is a powerful part of the joyful life of abiding in Christ.

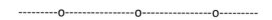

Dear Jesus, Thank You for loving me and suffering and dying for me, and for rising again from the dead for me. I love You and I want to follow You. I want to be willing to do whatever You want me to do, because I love You. I know Your plans are good and Your rewards are great. I want to be surrendered to You. Help me to give my life for You, as You gave Your life for me. Fill me with Your love for others. Help me to follow You. What do You want me to do? In Your name I pray, Amen.

9

Abiding in Him

"Abide in Me, and I in you…These things I have spoken to you, that My joy may remain in you, and that your joy may be full."

- John 15:4, 11

There is a big difference between a boat and a fish. A boat is in the water but it floats at the top, with the goal of having as little as possible of the water inside the boat. A fish is different. It doesn't just float on the water's surface- it is completely submerged in the water and the water that's inside the fish is critical to the life of the fish. God doesn't want us to be like boats- He wants us to be like fish. He wants us to be so immersed in Him, and to have so much of Himself in us, that He alone is our life. As Paul said, "To live is Christ."[1]

You might say this chapter is the heart of this book. Joy comes from abiding in Christ. In John Chapter 15, Jesus talks about us abiding in Him, and then says, "These things I have spoken to you, that My joy may remain in you, and that your joy may be full."[2] That's what God wants for us and that's what we all want- to have fullness of joy- His joy. The key to having His joy is to live a life that is centered on God, to live a life of abiding in Christ. So how do we do that?

---

[1] Philippians 1:21
[2] John 15:11

Perspectives

First, we need to have a right perspective of God and ourselves. We need to know that God is a Holy, Awesome, Righteous, All-powerful, Loving, Merciful and Wonderful God. We need to know that we are sinners in need of God's grace and mercy. We need to know that even though God is an Absolutely Righteous Judge, and will judge sin, He has chosen to show us mercy and has already judged our sins in Jesus. We need to know that Jesus suffered and died to pay the penalty for every sin we have ever committed and every sin we ever will commit, and that He rose again from the dead. We need to realize that Almighty God has promised that we are going to Heaven as a result of Jesus' absolute sacrifice and that Heaven is a better place than we could ever imagine. So, the first thing we need is to have right perspectives. Hopefully, this book has been a help in providing (or reminding you of) those right perspectives.

Preoccupations

Secondly, we need to have right preoccupations. What is a preoccupation? It is the act of engaging our mind, our energy, and our attention on something so much that it excludes other things. In other words, it's our total focus- it consumes and drives who we are. Our preoccupation is tied into our perspectives. If we really believe that God is Almighty, All-powerful, All-knowing, Righteous, Gracious, Loving and Merciful, and that we are sinners, saved by His amazing grace; it will affect our lives. In fact, it will radically affect our lives. If you were a totally in-love, 21 year old, and 10 minutes from now you were going to walk up to the altar to be married to the love of your life, what would you be thinking about? How you need to stop by the grocery store sometime next week to pick up some broccoli? Not likely. Your thoughts would be almost completely centered on the event that will take place in 10 minutes. "Am I ready?" "What will it be like?" "Is my fiancé excited?" "Exactly what will our wedding be like?" "What will it be like standing at the altar with my love?" You would be "preoccupied" with your spouse and your imminent wedding.

The writer of Hebrews tells us what our life-changing preoccupation should be. He says we should be "looking unto Jesus," and as we noted earlier, the word "looking" in this verse means, "to continually stare with awe and admiration." We should fix our minds, not on ourselves or on the things of this world, but we need to fix our minds continually on "the things above"[3]- on Jesus, "the author and perfecter of our faith."[4] As Isaiah the prophet wrote, "You will keep him in perfect peace, whose mind is stayed on You."[5] So how do we keep our minds "stayed" or "fixed" on Him?

Practices

Abiding in Christ involves our perspectives, our preoccupations and it has a lot to do with our practices- what we do. There are many verses in the Bible that give us wisdom and direction in what our practices should be, and we know some of them so well, we can almost say them in our sleep. But do we do them? The Scriptures warn, "be doers of the word, and not hearers only, deceiving yourselves."[6] What we do when we wake up in the morning, what we do right before we go to sleep, and what we do in between those two times, makes all the difference.

> There are many verses in the Bible that give us wisdom and direction in what our practices should be, and we know some of them so well, we can almost say them in our sleep. But do we do them?

Over the years, I have been blessed to be able to help some people by giving them counsel. After talking with a

---

[3] Colossians 3:2
[4] Hebrews 12:2 (NASB)
[5] Isaiah 26:3
[6] James 1:22

number of people who were seeking counsel, I began to notice a trend. Person after person, in fact the majority of people seeking counsel, had the same answer to a question I asked them. The question was, "Have you been spending time in prayer and reading your Bible?" Time after time, the answer was, "No." It's no wonder they needed counsel.

Prayer

As Christians, each of our bodies is a temple of the Holy Spirit- God's Spirit indwells us[7]- we are His house.[8] That is a wonderful truth. And God tells us, "My house shall be called a house of prayer."[9] That statement should be one of the things that best describes our lives. If God was to describe you, would He say, "House of prayer"?

God speaks about us as His followers, saying, "Even them I will bring to My holy mountain, and make them joyful in My house of prayer..."[10] It's a wonderful promise that God will make us joyful as we spend time with Him in prayer. Jesus also associated prayer with joy, saying, "Until now you have asked nothing in My name. Ask, and you will receive, that your joy may be full."[11] God wants to give us fullness of joy, and prayer is a key to having that joy.

> God speaks about us as His followers, saying, "Even them I will bring to My holy mountain, and make them joyful in My house of prayer..."

The Scriptures exhort us, "Continue earnestly in prayer,"[12] or as another translation reads, "Devote yourselves to prayer."[13] We are told to "pray without ceasing."[14] James

---

[7] 1 Corinthians 6:19

[8] Ephesians 2:22; 1 Peter 2:4-5

[9] Isaiah 56:7; Matthew 21:13; Mark 11:17; Luke 19:46

[10] Isaiah 56:7

[11] John 16:24

[12] Colossians 4:2

[13] Colossians 4:2 (NASB)

tells us, "You do not have because you do not ask."[15] Think about it- how can we possibly abide in Christ without being people of prayer? If God was to be compared to an ocean, would it be more accurate to describe you as a fish or a boat? Are you abiding in Him, or just floating on the surface? Prayer is essential in making the difference.

I'm not "Mr. Prayer Warrior." I certainly haven't arrived. But as I mentioned earlier in this book- disciplining myself for the purpose of godliness in the area of prayer, changed my life. And if it hasn't already changed your life, if you are willing to make the sacrifice and let Him lead you in it, it will change your life as well.

We say we want to follow Jesus and be like Him. Jesus was a man of prayer. But prayer is probably the most neglected area of many Christians' lives. Those who are only a little *with* God, will only be a little *for* God. God wants to do awesome things in and through our lives. If we want to be like the great missionary William Carey, who said, "Expect great things from God. Attempt great things for God," and if we want to abide in Christ, then we need to be people of prayer. You and I, like the disciples, should say, "Lord, teach us to pray,"[16]

> **If God was to be compared to an ocean, would it be more accurate to describe you as a fish or a boat? Are you abiding in Him, or just floating on the surface? Prayer is essential in making the difference.**

and then we should take some steps toward becoming "a house of prayer," so that God can fulfill His promise to make us "joyful in His house of prayer."

Prospering Through His Word

In the first Psalm, God says if we avoid listening to the counsel of, and practicing the sins of unbelievers, and we

---

[14] 1Thessalonians 5:17
[15] James 4:2
[16] Luke 11:1

instead meditate (reflect) on His Word, that we "shall be like a tree planted by the rivers of water, that brings forth its fruit in its season, whose leaf also shall not wither; and whatever he does shall prosper." Wow! Would you like that? To bear fruit at the perfect time and to have everything you do prosper? It sounds too good to be true. It sounds too easy. Does God really mean that? Yes. God means what He says. In speaking of us abiding in Christ, Jesus said if you "abide in Me, and My words abide in you, ask what you desire, and it shall be done for you."[17] Really? We can have whatever we want if we are abiding in Him and His words are abiding in us? Yes, because if we are abiding in Him and His words are abiding in us, He will be filling us with His Spirit and we will want what He wants- the very best.

I have a Christian friend who once said to me, "I already read the Bible once. I know what it says." He had no idea about the unfathomable riches he was missing out on by not regularly reading God's Word. Jesus said, "If you abide in My word, you are My disciples indeed. And you shall know the truth, and the truth shall make you free."[18] He also said, "The words that I speak to you are spirit, and they are life."[19]

> **If we are abiding in Him and His words are abiding in us, He will be filling us with His Spirit and we will want what He wants- the very best.**

Do you want to know the truth and be truly free? Do you want to really live life to the fullest? Yes? Then you need His Word. You need to read your Bible. Jesus said, "Man shall not live by bread alone, but by every word that proceeds from the mouth of God."[20] He related the Word of God to food. We live on food- we eat it several times a day. But Jesus said that's not enough. He said we also need "every word that proceeds from the mouth of God." Jesus is

---

[17] John 15:7

[18] John 8:31-32

[19] John 6:63

[20] Matthew 4:4

God,[21] and He says we should live on His Word. We need to take it in regularly, just like food. As was mentioned earlier in this book, we need to regularly and prayerfully read God's Word, seeking to hear what Almighty God might say to us and teach us through it.

Jesus said, "And this is eternal life, that they may know You, the only true God, and Jesus Christ whom You have sent."[22] So eternal life consists of knowing God the Father and Jesus Christ. We don't want to just know about God- we want to know God. The way we get to know someone is by spending time with them, and by interacting with them. As we spend time in prayer (not only talking, but listening as well), and spend time reading the Bible (with a listening heart), we will be interacting with God, getting to know Him. That's the heart of the matter. True Christianity is not a religion- it's a relationship. And spending time in prayer and His Word, are vital parts of that relationship- vital to really knowing Him and abiding in Him. Do we want to be like boats or fish?

The Bible also tells us, "whatever things were written before were written for our learning, that we through the patience and comfort of the Scriptures might have hope."[23] Do you want to grow in your understanding? Do you want comfort and hope? We can get them through the Scriptures. Paul said, "All Scripture is given by inspiration of God, and is profitable for doctrine, for reproof, for correction, for instruction in righteousness, that the man of God may be complete, thoroughly equipped for every good work."[24] Do you want to be profited by having right instruction and direction? Do you want maturity in your life? Do you want to be equipped for whatever you'll face? The psalmist writes, "Your word is a lamp to my feet and a light to my path."[25] We

---

[21] John 1:1

[22] John 17:3

[23] Romans 15:4

[24] 2 Timothy 3:16-17

[25] Psalm 119:105

need His Word to be our lamp (so we can understand the situations we're in) and our light (so we can know which way to go). "The word of God is living and powerful."[26] If you are not regularly spending time prayerfully reading the Bible, you are missing out on a "living and powerful" source of comfort, direction and joy in your life.

People of Faith

There is something else every one of us needs in order to abide in Christ and to live in joy. We need each other- we need other Christians. We are members of the body of Christ. The Scriptures say we should not be "forsaking our own assembling together, as is the habit of some, but encouraging one another; and all the more as you see the day drawing near."[27] One of the ways we run with joy as we run the Christian race is by having other Christians alongside of us to encourage us, and for us to encourage them.

The idea of a knee cap, an earlobe or an artery, being able to function without other members of the human body is ridiculous. Can you imagine a knee saying, to an artery, "I don't need you."? No, but somehow we think as Christians we can make it on our own. We think, "I've got God. Who else do I need?" God says we need each other. In the previous chapter, we looked at how essential love is in

> "Let us do good to all, especially to those who are of the household of faith." - Galatians 6:10

living a life of joy. Loving our neighbor is essential, and loving other Christians is even more essential. As Paul says, "let us do good to all, especially to those who are of the household of faith."[28] The Apostle John said, "he who does not love his brother whom he has seen, how can he love God whom he has not seen?"[29] Jesus said, "By this all will know that you are My

---

[26] Hebrews 4:12
[27] Hebrews 10:25
[28] Galatians 6:10
[29] 1 John 4:20

disciples, if you have love for one another."[30] Those verses (along with at least 50 more in the New Testament) are all talking about us loving other Christians.

Paul spends the first three chapters in the book of Ephesians speaking about the incredible spiritual blessings God has given us. Then in the fourth chapter, he speaks about what our response to God's amazing grace should be. He says, "I, therefore, the prisoner of the Lord, beseech you to walk worthy of the calling with which you were called, with all lowliness and gentleness, with longsuffering, bearing with one another in love, endeavoring to keep the unity of the Spirit in the bond of peace.

> God wants to fill you with His joy, and one of the ways He will do that is by loving you through other people and by loving other people through you.

There is one body and one Spirit, just as you were called in one hope of your calling; one Lord, one faith, one baptism; one God and Father of all, who is above all, and through all, and in you all."[31] Paul goes on and on speaking about how we should love one another and walk in unity. Why? Because that's God's heart. Just as God loves each of us so much, He also wants to love us through each other.

God wants to fill you with His joy, and one of the ways He will do that is by loving you through other people and by loving other people through you. It's one of the wonderful ways He works in our lives. We see in the book of Acts, that when God poured out His Spirit, people "were continually devoting themselves to... fellowship."[32] As we seek to abide in Him, we need to be people who are devoted to fellowship-people who are abiding in the body of Christ. We shouldn't just be going to church- we should *be* the church- by sharing our lives with other Believers. It's an important part of living a life of joy.

---

[30] John 13:35
[31] Ephesians 4:1-6
[32] Acts 2:42 (NASB)

The Prize

So much of what people do is for the purpose of getting something else. People go to school so they can get an education, so they can get a good job, so they can make money, so they can live comfortable lives, so they can be happy. They are working for the prize, the end goal. As Christians, we too can spend our lives doing things for the purpose of getting other things, so we can get the prize- our end goal. And it is good to work toward goals. But in reality, we already have the prize- it's God.

> **As we seek to abide in Him, we need to be people who are devoted to fellowship- people who are abiding in the body of Christ.**

What else could be better? What could be more fulfilling? What could satisfy us more than Him? What could be sweeter, richer, finer, more beautiful, more thrilling, more exhilarating, more awesome, more precious, more pure, or could result in more peace, comfort or joy than Him? What else do we need? There is nothing anywhere in existence that is better than God. Nothing has ever existed or will ever exist that is better or more desirable than God. The psalmist writes, "Whom have I in heaven but You? And there is none upon earth that I desire besides You. My flesh and my heart fail; but God is the strength of my heart and my portion forever."[33] He is everything worth desiring and we already have Him.

Then why is it that we are always looking for more? Why do so many of us spend so much time and energy pursuing other things? Like someone who has been wandering in a hot desert for weeks, who is dying of thirst, standing with parched lips at the shore of a giant lake of crystal clear, pure water, but who looks off into the distance at a mirage, trying to find something that will quench their thirst, we look off into the distance. "Maybe that over there will satisfy. Maybe if I can

---

[33] Psalm 73:25-26

just get that, or become that, or get her, or him, or be like her or him. Maybe when... Maybe if I can just..."

The list goes on and on as we think of those things that could quench our thirst and bring us joy. And yet the lake of crystal clear, pure water is right in front of us, waiting for us to drink. It is a paradox. Even though we have Him, we must also choose to seek

> We already have the prize- it's God. What else could be better? What could satisfy us more than He can?

Him. Like the man at the shore of the lake, we must choose to drink. That is the only way to quench our thirst.

The Pursuit

We will never be satisfied by the things of this world- not truly satisfied. If we are willing to take our minds off of "the cares of this world, the deceitfulness of riches, and the desires for other things,"[34] if we are willing to forego "the passing pleasures of sin,"[35] and to instead seek God, we will find riches indeed. As the psalmist writes, "As the deer pants for the water brooks, so pants my soul for You, O God. My soul thirsts for God, for the living God."[36] As we spend time seeking God in prayer, in His Word, and in fellowship with other believers; as we spend time praising Him, thanking Him, adoring Him, and serving Him, we will experience the greatest thing of all- God Himself. As A.W. Tozer wrote, "What I am anxious to see in Christian believers is a beautiful paradox. I want to see in them the joy of finding God while at the same time they are blessedly pursuing Him. I want to see in them the great joy of having God yet always wanting Him."[37]

---

[34] Mark 4:19

[35] Hebrews 11:25

[36] Psalm 42:1-2

[37] Men Who Met God, Christianity Today, v. 31, n. 1.

We are all pursuing things in this life, even if it's just pursuing peace by doing nothing- we are all heading in one direction or another. Whether we end up becoming victims or victors along the way depends on what we are pursuing. Let's run the race so as to receive the prize.[38] "Let us run with endurance the race that is set before us, looking unto Jesus, the author and finisher of our faith, who for the joy that was set before Him endured the cross, despising the shame, and has sat down at the right hand of the throne of God."[39] The rewards for our grand pursuit are awesome if we are pursuing God.

> "What I am anxious to see in Christian believers is a beautiful paradox. I want to see in them the joy of finding God while at the same time they are blessedly pursuing Him. I want to see in them the great joy of having God yet always wanting Him."
> - A.W. Tozer

His Presence

As King David writes, "In Your presence is fullness of joy; At Your right hand are pleasures forevermore."[40] As we have explored in this book, there will be a time for us who are trusting in the Lord, when we will see Him face to face, and we will know His joy in a way we have never imagined. But even today, as we go through life, we can know His presence- we can commune with Him. He is the "Lord of glory,"[41] and He is our "friend."[42] He is "high and lifted up"[43] and He is "God with us."[44] He is right there with you, right now, and He loves you.

> He is the Lord of glory, and He is our friend. He is high and lifted up and He is "God with us." He is right there with you, right now, and He loves you.

---

[38] 1 Corinthians 9:24
[39] Hebrews 12:1
[40] Psalm 16:11
[41] 1 Corinthians 2:8

There is nothing sweeter in this life than fellowship with God. There is no greater treasure. There is nothing that can satisfy you like His presence. There is no one that will ever love you more than He does. The key to life is to have an intimate relationship with the God who created intimacy.

Pauses

An interesting thing about pursuing God and seeking His presence is the value of pausing. It's not a mad rush to find God- He's right here with us. He says, "Be still, and know that I am God."[45] A lot of the time, we miss enjoying His presence because we are always involved in activity. Sometimes we need to get away from the business of life. In fact, hopefully it's every day that we choose to get alone and be still, and be quiet before our God. And hopefully, throughout the day, we are pausing to listen, pausing just to be sensitive to what His Spirit might say to us or how He might guide us- pausing to know that He is "God with us."

> Hopefully, throughout the day, we are pausing to listen, pausing just to be sensitive to what His Spirit might say to us or how He might guide us- pausing to know that He is "God with us."

Being in His presence is about us pouring out our hearts to God, it's about hearing God, and it's also about just being with Him. Abiding in Christ is not about striving and struggling and trying to get more *from* God. It's about resting in Him and getting more *of* God. In my first book, *How to Know the Will of God*, I relate a story of a time when I was on an early morning walk, talking with God and asking Him to speak to me. After a long time of silence, waiting for the Lord to put something on my heart, the Lord spoke to me and said, "I just want to be with you." It was life-changing for me. I

---

[42] John 15:15

[43] Isaiah 6:1

[44] Matthew 1:23

[45] Psalm 46:10

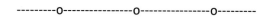

couldn't believe that the God who created the universe just wants to spend time with me. I was amazed. He is a God of intimacy. He is a God who loves just being with me, and He is a God who loves just being with you. He is the Shepherd who wants to guide you "beside the still waters,"[46] where He wants to restore your soul.[47] He is the God in whose presence, you will find "times of refreshing."[48] He wants to abide in you and for you to abide in Him- that you might have fullness of joy.

There are times in every one of our lives however, when we are in a valley, when all we can see when we try to look up, are dark clouds. As we will see in the next chapter; even in the deepest of valleys, we can still have joy- and it's easier to do than we might think.

---------o----------------o----------------o---------

Heavenly Father, Thank You for being such an awesome God. Please give me right perspectives about You, about myself, about others, and about the world. Please give me that Divine preoccupation, so that my focus on You and the things of Heaven will radically impact my life. Help me to discipline myself for the purpose of godliness. Please Lord, help me to become a house of prayer. Help me to learn how to abide in You. Help me to abide in Your Word and to allow Your Word to abide in me. Help me to be serious about sharing my life with other Christians. Help me to seek You and Your presence and help me to sit at Your feet. Help me to listen to You. In Jesus' name I pray, Amen.

---

[46] Psalm 23:2
[47] Psalm 23:3
[48] Acts 3:19

10

Joy in the Valley- Part I

"Though the fig tree may not blossom, nor fruit be on the vines; Though the labor of the olive may fail, and the fields yield no food; Though the flock may be cut off from the fold, and there be no herd in the stalls- Yet I will rejoice in the LORD, I will joy in the God of my salvation. The LORD God is my strength; He will make my feet like deer's feet, and He will make me walk on my high hills."

- Habakkuk 3:17-19

We all go through valleys- times of extreme trials when we can't help but wish there was some way to get out of our situations. Sometimes we feel like we are at the bottom- in a place where we can't get any lower. It could be because of the loss of a loved one, trouble we've gotten ourselves into, health problems, relationship problems, financial difficulties, guilt, pain inflicted on us by others, fear, feelings of worthlessness, loneliness, depression, or a combination of these things. If you've never had trials in your life- you will. Jesus said, "In the world you will have tribulation."[1] You may feel utterly alone in your trial. You may feel like nobody knows the pain you are going though, and there is no end in sight. But one of the blessings of being a Christian is that even though we go through trials, and sometimes they are severe, we do not "sorrow as others who have no hope."[2]

---

[1] John 16:33
[2] 1 Thessalonians 4:13

Dirty Windows

I was cleaning windows recently on the inside of a large home in Washington State. The woman who owned the home (I'll call her "T") seemed very troubled and unhappy. I noticed a few things in the home that indicated she was a Christian. I asked her if she was a Christian and she hesitated in her answer. She said she was a Christian but her daughter died a couple of years ago and she had been struggling in her relationship with God. It may be that there is no greater grief a person can endure than to lose a child. I saw pictures of T's daughter around the home. She looked like a warm-hearted, happy girl. She was probably a wonderful person.

I believe the Lord allowed me to feel some of T's pain over the loss of her precious daughter. As Christians, we want to come alongside those who are hurting, to comfort them. I tried to tell T that God loves her. I wanted her to know that the fact that her daughter died doesn't mean that God doesn't love her and it doesn't matter how angry we are at God, He still loves us. Several times, I tried to speak the words but every time I tried to say something, I started crying. I got choked up with emotion and I just couldn't get the words out. Her pain was so deep and so severe. I can't imagine what it's like to bear that pain every day. I don't know what it's like to lose a child I've loved. I've never had children of my own. I don't know exactly what it's like to be in the valley that T is in, or that you may be in- but God does.

> I don't know exactly what it's like to be in the valley you may be in- but God does.

He knows exactly what it's like to lose a child whom He loves dearly. He knows exactly what it's like to be in any storm or valley that we may go through- and He cares. He cares deeply. When Lazarus died, Jesus wept for his sisters Martha and Mary, and for the others who were grieving over the loss of Lazarus.[3] Jesus felt their pain and He grieved for them, and

---

[3] Matthew 11:33,35

Jesus hasn't changed. "Jesus Christ is the same yesterday, today, and forever."[4] He feels your pain and knows your fears and He cares. He knows everything you go through. As a shepherd of God's people, the Apostle Paul said, "what comes upon me daily: my deep concern for all the churches. Who is weak, and I am not weak?"[5] Paul had a "deep concern" for people, but Jesus is the Great Shepherd of our souls and He cares far more than anyone on earth

> **God cares about every sparrow that falls to the ground- and He cares far more about you.**

does about you and what you go through. Jesus said God cares about every sparrow that falls to the ground-[6] and He cares far more about you.[7]

Why Does God Allow Suffering?

Of course, the question that comes to mind is, "Then why does God allow suffering? We are His children. If He knows how much it hurts, if He knows how fearful we become, if He knows how long and how severe our hardships are, and if He cares, then why in the world does He allow it?" The reality is that like T, we all have dirty windows- we can't see everything now like we want to. As the Apostle Paul says, "For now we see in a mirror, dimly, but then face to face. Now I know in part, but then I shall know just as I also am known."[8] In the Bible, God tells us some of the reasons He allows suffering. It can be comforting to know some of them but when we are going through a valley or storm, the most important thing is not to know why. The most important thing is to hold tight to Jesus- the One who is in the storm with us, the One who knows and cares what we are going through, the One who can

---

[4] Hebrews 13:8
[5] 2 Corinthians 11:28
[6] Matthew 10:29
[7] Matthew 10:31
[8] 1 Corinthians 13:12

get us across to the other side, the One who walked through a deeper valley than we ever will.

Looking Down the Road

It is very difficult for us, especially when we are in a valley or storm, to be able to look at the big picture. We see the steep valley walls, the dark foreboding shadows, and we can't see the sun. We see the raging surf, the waves smashing against the rocks and the hurricane force winds, and we ask why. All we can see is what's right in front of us and right behind us. We can't see the future. While we can't know all the answers now, one thing we can know for certain is that if you were in God's place- if you were all-knowing and perfectly loving and merciful, you would allow exactly what He is allowing in your life. His ways are perfect.[9] He is love,[10] and again, He truly cares.[11] It is very reasonable for us to wonder why God allows suffering. But when we face suffering, the most important thing is not that we know and lean on the one reason for our suffering; it's that we know and lean on the One Risen for our suffering. Much of the time when we are going through trials, God is not asking us to understand what He is doing- He's asking us to trust Him. He wants us to "walk by faith, not by sight."[12]

> **When we face suffering, the most important thing is not that we know and lean on the one reason for our suffering; it's that we know and lean on the One Risen for our suffering.**

But Why?

In the beginning there was no suffering. There was no pain, no fear, and no death. Then sin came into the world. Adam and Even turned away from trusting God and His

---

[9] Psalm 18:30

[10] 1 John 4:8,16

[11] 1 Peter 5:7

[12] 2 Corinthians 5:7

Word, and chose the way of pride and selfishness. God must have been very grieved as He asked the question of Adam, the question He already knew the answer to- "Where are you?" The separation from God that Adam and Eve were experiencing was just the beginning of thousands of years of suffering, pain and death. Notice that it wasn't God's doing. Because God is love, He gave Adam and Eve freedom of choice. Adam and Eve chose the path of sin. One thing we can absolutely know when we are suffering- it's not God's fault. It was when sin entered the world that suffering began.

You might ask, "If suffering was brought into the world through sin, why doesn't God just wipe out sin, and why didn't He wipe it out in the garden?" Good question, but you might not like the answer. If God was to wipe out sin, Adam and Eve would have been killed immediately. And every person who has been born since Adam and Eve (including you and I) would never have been born. Even as people

> One thing we can absolutely know when we are suffering- it's not God's fault.

who seek to honor God and follow Christ, you and I sin every day. As the Apostle John says, "If we say that we have no sin, we deceive ourselves, and the truth is not in us."[13] We live in a "fallen world." All of us fall short.[14] If God was to wipe out sin, you and I wouldn't stand a chance. You might ask, "Well, if God is all-powerful, then why doesn't He at least protect Christians from the results of sin while we are on this earth, or at least protect people from suffering they didn't cause?" A baby is born with a severe birth defect, a woman is raped, or a child is born into an abusive family. We wonder why God would allow it.

If we want to consider the ultimate case of an innocent person suffering, it would be Jesus Christ. He was perfectly innocent. He was tempted to sin, over and over, in all the

---

[13] 1 John 1:8
[14] Romans 3:23

ways we are tempted, but He never once gave in- He never once committed a sin.[15] And yet He suffered an excruciatingly painful death. He never did anything wrong, but He suffered more than you and I can imagine. Of course, we know He suffered for a perfectly good reason- to pay the penalty for our sins- because God is love. As we looked at earlier in this book, because God is perfectly good, He is a God of absolute perfect justice. Every sin ever committed will be judged and paid for. I am so thankful that my sins were paid for on the cross- that as Jesus hung there, bloody, beaten and in agony- as He died, He said, "It is finished,"[16] which could also be translated as "paid in full." He paid for every one of our sins.

We now look back at His suffering and we thank God for it. We are grateful that Jesus was willing to endure suffering for our sake. The ultimate in innocence endured the ultimate in suffering, for you and me. We can look back

> **The ultimate in innocence endured the ultimate in suffering, for you and me.**

and see how wonderful and merciful our Heavenly Father is to give His only begotten Son to suffer for us, and we can see how loving and merciful it was for Jesus to willingly give His life for us.

They Didn't Understand

But two thousand years ago, it wasn't so clear. As Jesus hung there in agony, He cried out, "My God, My God, why have You forsaken Me?"[17] Jesus didn't understand why God was allowing Him to suffer the way He was. And can you imagine how those who were close to Jesus felt when He was crucified? He was the perfect embodiment of love. He was the wisest, most caring person who had ever lived- and His murderers spat in His face, beat Him mercilessly and nailed Him to a cross to suffer in shame until He died. Those who

---

[15] Hebrews 4:15
[16] John 17:30
[17] Matthew 27:46

were close to Jesus lost the most wonderful person they had ever known; in fact, they lost the most wonderful person to ever walk the face of the earth. They also lost their hope. They thought Jesus was the Messiah, the Savior and hope of their nation and the world- now He was dead.

But they didn't understand. God had a reason for allowing Jesus' suffering- a perfectly good reason. And God has reasons for allowing our suffering- perfectly good reasons. In time, those who knew Jesus and were grieving so much over His death, saw that indeed, God's plans are perfect and His ways are good. Now they can look back and see that God allowed horrible things to happen in order for good things to be the result. In the same way, we will in time be

> **God had a perfectly good reason for allowing Jesus' suffering- and God has perfectly good reasons for allowing our suffering.**

able to look back and see that God allowed horrible things to happen in our lives in order for good things to be the result. "And we know that all things work together for good to those who love God, to those who are the called according to His purpose.[18] We will look back on things that baffle our minds now, and say, "God, Your ways are truly perfect."

In the meantime, we need to choose to lean on Him and to trust Him. When we don't understand what is happening, it is critical that we stand on three things we know- 1- God is good. 2- We are not alone- God is with us. And 3- God's Word is true.

A Broken Family

My grandfather was successful in business. He and my grandmother were able to buy a house on the side of Diamond Head, an exclusive area in Honolulu, Hawaii. In 1941, on the night after Christmas, my grandfather, having just come downstairs after scolding my mother and her brother for

---

[18] Romans 8:28

playing with a toy he had told them not to play with, sat down in a chair and had a heart attack and died. He was 38 years old. My mother was only eight.

My mother's family went into a tailspin. My grandmother was suddenly a grieving widow and a single mother raising three children. It was just a few weeks after the attack on Pearl Harbor and the country was at war. My mother and her brother blamed themselves for my grandfather's death. Life was difficult. My grandmother tried to comfort them by telling them that God needed their father more than they did, so He took him to Heaven.

My uncle started getting into trouble and acting out in school and was expelled. My mother grew up thinking that either God was mean, or that she was responsible for her father's death. Her family had been on the fast track to a life of comfort and ease. Why would God allow such a tragedy? It's now been almost 75 years since my grandfather's death and I can't say I know all the answers, but I can look back and make some observations.

My grandfather's early death prevented my family from becoming very wealthy. If I was born into a wealthy family, I might have grown up spoiled and self-sufficient. Jesus said it's difficult for a rich man to enter the Kingdom of Heaven.[19] I have always been a fairly stubborn person. Had I grown up rich, it might be that I would have been far more resistant to the Gospel. The (relative) poverty that I grew up in (my parents were divorced when I was five years old and my single mother raised four of us children, often working for minimum wage) may be something the Lord used to help soften my heart.

I received the Lord when I was 30 years old. Since then I have been blessed to be used by the Lord to help lead my grandmother and my uncle (and others in my family) to a saving relationship with Jesus. I believe my grandmother and

---

[19] Matthew 19:23; Mark 10:25; Luke 18:25

uncle are now in Heaven for eternity. There are also other people who God has used me to help save. I'm sure those whom I have prayed for or led to Christ, have also prayed for others and led others to Christ. And those people have prayed for and helped lead others to Christ. It may be that by the time I get to Heaven, I may have been used by God to help hundreds or thousands of people to know of His love and mercy.

I believe my grandmother and uncle are now in Heaven and that they now have very "clean windows." They can see how God worked through a tragedy to impact lives for eternity. Were the years of suffering and hardship worth it? I believe my grandmother, uncle and thousands of other people won't be asking God why he allowed it. Instead, they will be saying, "God, Your ways are truly perfect."

It Can Help to Know Why

We won't know all of the reasons why God allows certain things to happen in our lives until we get to Heaven, but God does tell us some of the reasons now. One of the reasons God allows suffering in our lives is to make us more like our Lord and Savior. We are told that Jesus was made perfect "through sufferings."[20] Through His suffering, He could truly understand what it is like to endure suffering- because He's been there. We can't say, "God, You have no idea what I'm going through," because He does- He knows exactly what we're going through, and Jesus is with us in all of our trials, whether we know it or not. (It can help a lot if we

> By going through times of suffering, we develop compassion for others who are suffering, and are able to come alongside and comfort them with the comfort with which we ourselves are comforted by God.

---

[20] Hebrews 2:10

know it.) Just as He knows about every sparrow that falls to the ground[21] and the number of hairs on your head,[22] He knows your every thought and concern. He knows your pain, sorrow and fears.

By going through times of suffering, we develop compassion for others who are suffering, and are able to come alongside and comfort them. God is the One "who comforts us in all our tribulation, that we may be able to comfort those who are in any trouble, with the comfort with which we ourselves are comforted by God."[23] When we are in a valley, storm or fire, it may not seem worth it to us- we can think, "What? I'm going through this so I can have my faith strengthened and help others?! There's got to be a better way!" But God knows what the future holds. He knows how He will be able to use us in the future to bless others, because of what we have suffered.

Take for example, a woman whose child has died. The pain of the loss is more than many of us can imagine. But if you could see the future (like God can) and see that she will eventually be able to come alongside and comfort another woman (or two or three or more) who has lost a child, and maybe even help her to come to a saving knowledge of Christ, your perspective changes. The woman she leads to Christ may (pray for and/or) lead several others to Christ. And they may lead others to Christ. There may be many people in Heaven for eternity, in part because of the first woman who lost a child (who is now in Heaven) and she was willing to be used by God to comfort others with the comfort God comforted her with. In Heaven, that woman will look back and see how God caused all things to work together for the good of those who love Him- and she will praise God. Soon after her loss, it may be impossible for her to imagine ever praising God for

---

allowing her child to die, but in time, she will see things in a new light.

I have been through storms and valleys in my life and it was when I was at my lowest, that Jesus met me in a way that showed me that He is with me walking through the valleys and storms, even though I can't see Him, and most of the time, can't feel Him. Those experiences strengthened my faith and help assure me that He is truly with us in our valleys, and they help me to be able to comfort others with the comfort with which I was comforted.

The Apostle James wrote, "My brethren, count it all joy when you fall into various trials, knowing that the testing of your faith produces patience. But let patience have its perfect work, that you may be perfect and complete, lacking nothing."[24] We all want to have patience. It's a fruit of the Holy Spirit.[25] We say, "I want patience and I want it now!" But patience doesn't always come easily, and it often takes time- much longer than we want to wait. As James says, it comes through trials and the testing of our faith. As we wait on God to come through for us, and then in time (sometimes it seems like a very long time) He does, our faith is strengthened. We realize again that God is faithful. He is with us and He always keeps His promises. And sometimes we also realize that we put ourselves through more suffering than we needed to go through, because we weren't trusting God and leaning on Him and His promises- instead, we were worrying and grieving. That's why James says to "count it all joy." We can choose to have joy in trials, knowing they will make us more like our Lord and Savior. It's a powerful truth- if you make the choice to surrender to God and say, "God, I choose to count it all joy when I fall into various trials, knowing that the testing of my faith produces patience," God will give you His joy in the trials.

---

[24] James 1:2-4
[25] Galatians 5:22 (NASB)

We see this in Paul's life. He tells about his "thorn in the flesh,"[26] and how he cried out to God repeatedly, asking Him to remove it. God's response to Paul was, "My grace is sufficient for you, for My strength is made perfect in weakness."[27] How did Paul take that? He said, "Therefore most gladly I will rather boast in my infirmities, that the power of Christ may rest upon me. Therefore, I take pleasure in infirmities, in reproaches, in needs, in persecutions, in distresses, for Christ's sake. For when I am weak, then I am strong."[28] He allowed God to give him strength, peace and joy. We, like Paul, can say, "I can do all things through Christ who strengthens me."[29]

Of course, it's not a sin to ever grieve or cry. There is "a time to weep."[30] Even Jesus cried,[31] and we should not feel guilty about going through times of grief and mourning, but we should not experience the same "sorrow as others who have no hope."[32] Our hope can cast a ray of sunshine on even

> **We should not experience the same "sorrow as others who have no hope." Our hope can cast a ray of sunshine on even our gloomiest of days.**

our gloomiest of days. And as the classic hymn, *What a Friend We Have in Jesus*, sings, "O what peace we often forfeit, O what needless pain we bear, all because we do not carry everything to God in prayer! Have we trials and temptations? Is there trouble anywhere? We should never be discouraged, take it to the Lord in prayer. Can we find a friend so faithful who will all our sorrows share? Jesus knows our every weakness, take it to the Lord in prayer. Are we weak and heavy-laden, cumbered

---

[26] 2 Corinthians 12:7
[27] 2 Corinthians 12:9
[28] 2 Corinthians 12:9-10
[29] Philippians 4:13
[30] Ecclesiastes 3:4
[31] John 11:35
[32] 1 Thessalonians 4:13

with a load of care? Precious Savior, still our refuge- take it to the Lord in prayer; do thy friends despise, forsake thee? Take it to the Lord in prayer; in His arms He'll take and shield thee, thou wilt find a solace there."

Back to reasons God allows suffering- James tells us we can rejoice when we face trials because they produce godly character in us- they develop patience and help us in maturing to be more like Christ. The Apostle Paul also gives us insights into reasons why God allows suffering. Paul said we "rejoice in hope of the glory of God. And not only that, but we also glory in tribulations, knowing that tribulation produces perseverance; and perseverance, character; and character, hope."[33] When Paul says we "rejoice in hope" and "glory in tribulation," the words "rejoice" and "glory" are the same word in the original language (Greek). It could be translated, we "rejoice in hope" and we "rejoice in tribulation."

Paul was a person who experienced a lot of tribulations- storms and valleys. Let's let him describe some of them in his own words- "...in far more labors, in far more imprisonments, beaten times without number, often in danger of death. Five times I received from the Jews thirty-nine lashes. Three times I was beaten with rods, once I was stoned, three times I was shipwrecked, a night and a day I have spent in the deep. I have been on frequent journeys, in dangers from rivers, dangers from robbers, dangers from my countrymen, dangers from the Gentiles, dangers in the city, dangers in the wilderness, dangers on the sea, dangers among false brethren; I have been in labor and hardship, through many sleepless nights, in hunger and thirst, often without food, in cold and exposure. Apart from such external things, there is the daily pressure on me of concern for all the churches. Who is weak without my being weak? Who is led into sin without my

---

[33] Romans 5:2-4

intense concern?"[34]   Paul also said he was "condemned to death... a spectacle to the world... without honor... poorly clothed... roughly treated... homeless... reviled... persecuted... slandered... as the scum of the world, the dregs of all things..."[35]

Paul had (in the words of an old saying) "been through the wringer." He couldn't even count the number of times he'd been beaten.[36] Have you ever thought about what it would be like to be beaten with rods, or to have an angry mob of people pick up rocks and try to kill you with them, or to spend years in prison on false charges, or to float in the ocean for a day and a night after having the ship you were on, sink? Those are just a few of the things Paul endured, and yet as he grew in his relationship with God, he reached a point where he could say, "I am exceedingly joyful in all our tribulation."[37] What? He was joyful as people threw rocks at his head, and as he was beaten with rods? Yes, because as he said, he rejoiced, "knowing that tribulation produces perseverance; and perseverance, character; and character, hope."[38]

Do We Want What God Wants?

Those are three things Paul desired for his life and we should desire them too- perseverance, character and hope. I don't want to be a quitter. I don't want to be a person of little character who doesn't have much hope- like one of those people Jesus described as "he who hears the word and immediately receives it with joy; yet he has no root in himself, but endures only for a while. For when tribulation or persecution arises because of the word, immediately he stumbles."[39]

---

[34] 2 Corinthians 11:23-29 (NASB)
[35] 1 Corinthians 4:9-13 (NASB)
[36] 2 Corinthians 11:23 (NASB)
[37] 2 Corinthians 7:4
[38] Romans 5:3-4
[39] Matthew 13:20-21

I want to be someone who perseveres, someone of good character, and someone with a lot of hope. We all go through trials and as they say, we can become bitter or become better as we go through them. Paul knew that no matter what he went through, it just made him focus more on the Lord and on Heaven- it gave Him more hope. Paul had learned the secret of turning his suffering upwards and of putting his focus on the One who suffered even more for him. Like Paul, we too can turn our suffering upwards. We can offer it as a sacrifice to the Lord and say, "Lord, I am willing to go through this for You." Paul was willing to suffer, and suffer a lot, in order to become more like our Wonderful Lord and Savior.

Paul said, "Therefore we do not lose heart. Even though our outward man is perishing, yet the inward man is being renewed day by day. For our light affliction, which is but for a moment, is working for us a far more exceeding and eternal weight of glory, while we do not look at the things which are seen, but at the things which are not seen. For the things which are seen are temporary,

> No matter what we go through in this life; we can always be looking forward to our future joy.

but the things which are not seen are eternal."[40] Paul was looking at something far beyond his pain. He was looking at the eternal. This is a key to enduring suffering- no matter what we go through in this life; we can always be looking forward to our future joy.

Job lost everything. All ten of his children were killed at once in a disaster. It's hard for any of us to imagine what that would be like. Many of us have read or heard that story numerous times but have never really thought about it. Think about what it would be like to have ten children and to have them all die at the same time. In addition to that, He lost his health, his wealth, his livestock, and all of his friends turned

---

[40] 2 Corinthians 4:16-18

on him. Even his wife said, "Curse God and die!"[41] And yet he said, "When He has tested me, I shall come forth as gold."[42] Job knew that God was testing and refining Him.[43] God was making Job more like Himself, and Job was willing to pay the price. As a result, millions of people have read or heard the story of Job and have been comforted because of what Job suffered- millions of people's lives have been blessed. God has probably used Job's trials to help bring many people to Heaven for eternity and has used his suffering to help many persevere in hard times. Now that he is in Heaven, Job can look back and say "As for God, His way is perfect."[44] What made absolutely no sense to Job at the time, makes perfect sense to him now.

Yet I Will Rejoice in the Lord

The prophet Habakkuk said, "Though the fig tree may not blossom, nor fruit be on the vines; though the labor of the olive may fail, and the fields yield no food; though the flock may be cut off from the fold, and there be no herd in the stalls-- Yet I will rejoice in the LORD, I will joy in the God of my salvation. The LORD God is my strength; He will make my feet like deer's feet, and He will make me walk on my high hills."[45]

Habakkuk was facing a truly dire situation. No figs and no grapes meant there would be no dried fruit to eat during the winter months. Not having olives meant not having the precious oil from the olives. The fields producing no food- that meant no wheat and no bread. Not having flocks and herds meant no sheep, goats or cattle and no milk. No food?

---

[41] Job 2:9

[42] Job 23:10

[43] God already knew Job's heart but the testing revealed to Job the condition of his own heart.

[44] Psalm 18:30

[45] Habakkuk 3:17-19

No oil? No animals? In ancient Israel, that meant disaster-total starvation.

Even when facing a disaster of this magnitude Habakkuk said he would rejoice in the Lord. Did he say he would rejoice because there was no food? Of course not. The idea of starving to death doesn't bring joy to anybody. We should never rejoice, saying, "That's great. I lost my home, or my job, or my spouse, or my health, or my parents, or my child, or my income." But Habakkuk's focus was on the Lord. And he said, "I will rejoice in the Lord." That word "rejoice" in the original language (Hebrew) is "aw-laz" which literally means "to jump for joy." He then says "I will joy in the God of my salvation." The Hebrew word for "joy" in that verse means, "To spin around under the influence of violent emotion," or "to leap for joy."

Notice what Habakkuk didn't say. He didn't describe how bad the situation was and then say, "But somehow we are going to get through this," or that he would have to just grin and bear it. He didn't just say, "Don't worry. Be happy." Notice that he also didn't deny what was going on. There are many false teachers today who say we need to just positively confess everything. They'll say, "I'm not sick. I don't have cancer," and then they'll die from cancer. Habakkuk is describing how bad the situation is, and how bad it looks for the near future, and then he turns a corner- a huge corner. He says, "Yet I will rejoice in the Lord..." It's sort of like someone saying, "I am completely broke and have no way to make an income, but I know that God is faithful. I will rejoice in Him. I'm going to Heaven!"

Notice that when Habakkuk mentioned the Lord, he also mentioned that He is the God of his salvation. We see another of so many examples of God's people finding joy by looking to the future, rather than dwelling on the circumstances of the present. I don't know exactly what you've been through, are going through right now, or will go through in the future, but I know the One who does. And He cares. So often, when we go through the storms, we can't understand why God would allow it- "If He loves me, why does He allow me to suffer like this? Why does it seem like nothing is going right?"

In Heaven, all of those questions will be answered, but for now, we can choose to trust Him. Even though we don't know all of the "whys," we know the "Who," and that's what matters. He is right there with you, whether you "feel" Him or not. He is the God who says, "I will never leave you nor forsake you."[46] He will always be with you, and He will always care about you. You can be "casting all your care upon Him, for He cares for you."[47] And you're going to Heaven!

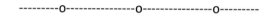

Father, I praise You because You are good. Thank You that no matter what I go through, You are with me. Whether I sense Your Holy Spirit comforting me and dwelling with me or not, Your promises are true- You haven't left me and You never will. Help me to think about You and Your promises, rather than dwelling on my trials. You are the God who cares about me. Help me Lord, not to blame You for what's happening in my life, or in the lives of those I care about. Your ways are perfect. Help me not to spend too much time wondering and questioning You as to why You allow certain things to happen. Help me to lean on You instead- to stop trying to lean on the one reason, and to lean on the One Risen. Help me to "consider it all joy" when I fall into various trials. Thank You that You've counted me worthy to be tested. God, You are faithful and You are good. I love You. In Jesus' name I pray, Amen.

---

[46] Hebrew 13:5
[47] 1 Peter 5:7

11

Joy in the Valley- Part II

"as sorrowful, yet always rejoicing."
- 2 Corinthians 6:10

What if Worse Comes to Worst?

We can all imagine some pretty horrible scenarios if we try. Of course, some of us have gone through, or are going through valleys or storms that many have never experienced. Let's look at a deep valley- a very deep valley, and examine it in the light of God's wisdom.

The United States is a wonderful nation. Many books have been written extolling its virtues. But the U.S. has declined morally over time. Many would say the U.S. is now ripe for God's judgment- that as a nation, we have turned our back on God (even though there are many people in the U.S. who are faithful and who love God). What if God were to judge the U.S.? What if for example, God was to allow radical Muslims to have their way in the U.S., in the same way that He allowed the Babylonians to invade Israel?

What if, God forbid, there was a group of terrorists (and this is actually reported to be one of their plans) that split up and travelled to different parts of the United States (or whatever country you live in)? What if they had 5 or 7 (or 15) suitcase-sized nuclear bombs, and they placed themselves in different cities around the country and one Monday morning, one of them detonated a nuclear bomb in the heart of New York City? And what if the next Monday, another terrorist set off another nuclear bomb in Los Angeles? The next week another one goes off in Boston, then Dallas, then Philadelphia, then San Diego, and then another one devastates a smaller city the next week?

Many thousands of people would be killed by the blasts, but the resulting chaos in our country could be far worse. What if people were fleeing cities all across the nation, not knowing if their city might be next? What if businesses closed, banks closed, and the economy collapsed? What if gas stations ran out of gas? What if, within a few days, grocery stores ran out of food? What if people were looting stores, and robbing and killing each other- it could result in mass starvation and utter chaos. Would it be possible to have even a tiny bit of joy in a situation like that? Can we really be "sorrowful, yet always rejoicing"[1]?

The Earthquake

A number of years ago, I had the privilege to talk with a Christian leader in India. Just shortly before our talking together, he had gone through an amazing experience. He was in the North Indian state of Gujarat on Friday morning, January 26th, 2001, when an earthquake measuring 7.7 on the Richter scale hit the state of Gujarat, killing over 20,000 people. The earthquake occurred at 8:40 in the morning and lasted for two minutes. When the earthquake hit, "Raj"[2] and other leaders from different Christian ministries were in a prayer meeting on the second floor of a two-story concrete building. As the building started to shake violently, the leaders ran to get out. The building was located next to a taller, four-story building and the only way out of the two-story building was down a stairway that exited underneath the four-story building.

Raj was in front of the rest of the group as they ran down the stairs. Raj said he was about an arm's length away from the door leading into the ground floor of the four-story

---

[1] 2 Corinthians 6:10

[2] His name has been changed for security purposes.

building, when the concrete four-story building collapsed. Several floors of thick concrete crashed to the ground just inches in front of Raj's face, completely blocking the exit. It was dark because of all the dust in the air. Raj couldn't see a thing and was certain he was about to die. He was trapped in a swaying concrete stairway which felt like it would collapse at any moment. As far as he knew, there was no way out. The building was shaking back and forth violently as he stood on the stairs in absolute pitch-black darkness.

What did Raj do? He raised both his hands and started shouting praises to God. He knew that in a moment he was going to be with the Lord. What an exciting moment! Wait a minute! As far as he knew, wasn't he about to die? Yes, but Raj knows that Heaven is a better place than the earth. Raj knows that Jesus

> **Raj knew he was about to die. He raised both his hands and started shouting praises to God.**

has prepared a place for Him. Raj knows that the best things on earth can't even begin to compare with the joys of Heaven- and Raj was ready to go Home.

He shouted praises to God and after a minute or so, the building stopped shaking. The concrete ceiling didn't come crashing down on him. As the people started feeling around in the darkness, one of them found a small window on a wall of the stairway. They were all able to climb out the window to safety, unharmed.

Raj was able to rejoice and experience great joy even in a terrible situation because he realized that he could be going to Heaven at any moment. And you know what? You and I could be going to Heaven at any moment as well. We have no guarantees that we will even be on this earth for another minute. The Lord could come back any second.

Shifting Our Focus

Sometimes it takes extreme situations to help us really shift our focus off of the things of this world, onto eternal things. God forbid, if our (or your) country was devastated by terrorism, war, plague or economic collapse. But you know what? God would still be faithful. His promises would still be true. And we could still have joy. Even though we would have a lot to cry about, a lot to grieve over, and a great number of things we could be worried about- we could still have an undercurrent of God's peace and joy in our lives. We can be "sorrowful, yet always rejoicing."[3]

Needless to say, our lives would be completely changed, and for many of us, we might only have a little time left on this earth. But life is short. We were never going to have all that long a time here anyway. And we deserve to be in Hell for eternity. That is the suffering every one of us deserves.

> No matter what we suffer in this life, it will be nothing compared to what we deserve.

No matter what we suffer in this life, it will be nothing compared to what we deserve. Jesus has already suffered for us. And we should be living with an eager expectancy of His return. We are going to a better place very soon- a much better place. As Solomon wrote, "To everything there is a season."[4] This trial will pass. Do you feel like you are walking through a deep, dark valley right now? "To everything there is a season." Are you going through a fire? "To everything there is a season." Are you in a storm? "To everything there is a season." It's temporary.

> No matter how bad it is, "To everything there is a season."

No matter how bad it is, "To everything there is a season." We can still finish strong. We can fix our eyes on Him and live each moment we have, with an eternal focus. Jesus said, "In the world you will have tribulation; but be of good cheer, I have overcome the world."[5] He has conquered sin. He has conquered evil. He has conquered suffering and pain and fear. He has conquered death. They exist in the

---

[3] 2 Corinthians 6:10
[4] Ecclesiastes 3:1
[5] John 16:33

world for a short time but they are already defeated foes. Their days are numbered. They only exist for "a season." Jesus loves us and He has overcome the world- we can be of good cheer.

It is so easy to fall into the trap of thinking we need Jesus plus... When you think about it- what do you really need? Do you need money? Do you need a place to live? Do you need food? Do you need water? Do you need your family, your children, your spouse or your friends? Do you need another day of life? Do you need your health or another breath of air? In reality, the answer to all of these questions, is "No." All you need is God. If you have Him, you have everything. If He chooses not to give you another breath, in just a few short seconds (if you have put your trust in Him) you will be in His presence, in fullness of joy.

As Paul says, "In this you greatly rejoice, though now for a little while, if need be, you have been grieved by various trials, that the genuineness of your faith, being much more precious than gold that perishes, though it is tested by fire, may be found to praise, honor, and glory at the revelation of Jesus Christ, whom having not seen you love. Though now you do not see Him, yet believing, you rejoice with joy inexpressible and full of glory."[6] We can "greatly rejoice" with "joy inexpressible"- our faith is proven to be genuine as it is "tested by fire," and it will result in "praise, honor and glory" when Jesus takes us to Heaven.

Persecution

Sometimes the reason we encounter trials is because we are doing things right- we are seeking to honor the Lord with our lives. As the Apostle Peter tells us, "Beloved, do not think it strange concerning the fiery trial which is to try you, as though some strange thing happened to you; but rejoice to the extent that you partake of Christ's sufferings, that when His

---

[6] 1 Peter 1:6-8

glory is revealed, you may also be glad with exceeding joy. If you are reproached for the name of Christ, blessed are you, for the Spirit of glory and of God rests upon you."[7] One of God's promises is that "all who desire to live godly in Christ Jesus will suffer persecution."[8] In fact, Jesus said, "Blessed are you when they revile and persecute you, and say all kinds of evil against you falsely for My sake. Rejoice and be exceedingly glad, for great is your reward in heaven."[9]

I think of that missionary I met in India, who had been beaten so badly for Christ, that his head had swollen up like a melon, whose eyes teared up with joy as he said, "I am so privileged to be beaten for Christ." He was "exceedingly glad" that he was counted worthy to suffer for Jesus. We are told that when we suffer because of our faith in Jesus, "rejoice to the extent that you partake of Christ's sufferings."[10] The more we suffer for Him, the more we should rejoice.

> "Rejoice to the extent that you partake of Christ's sufferings."
> - 1 Peter 4:13

The Shepherd's Rod

Of course, sometimes when we are in a storm or valley and we say, "God, what did I do to deserve this?" He answers us- because our difficulties might be a result of something we did or failed to do. God is a perfect Father. When we get out of line, He will correct us. His discipline, like the discipline of any good father, is not pleasurable for the moment. "'My son, do not despise the chastening of the LORD, nor be discouraged when you are rebuked by Him; for whom the LORD loves He chastens, and scourges every son whom He receives.' If you endure chastening, God deals with you as with sons; for what son is there whom a father does not

---

[7] 1 Peter 4:12-14
[8] 2 Timothy 3:12
[9] Matthew 5:11-12
[10] 1 Peter 4:13

chasten? But if you are without chastening, of which all have become partakers, then you are illegitimate and not sons. Furthermore, we have had human fathers who corrected us, and we paid them respect. Shall we not much more readily be in subjection to the Father of spirits and live? For they indeed for a few days chastened us as seemed best to them, but He for our profit, that we may be partakers of His holiness. Now no chastening seems to be joyful for the present, but painful; nevertheless, afterward it yields the peaceable fruit of righteousness to those who have been trained by it."[11]

God disciplines us because He loves us, and we need to be willing to accept His discipline. It is definitely for our own good and for the good of others. He sometimes uses trials to get us back on the right path. As the psalmist wrote, "Before I was afflicted I went astray, but now I keep Your word."[12]

Often times when we encounter trials, God doesn't immediately reveal the reasons He is allowing them in our lives, but one of the many great things about God is that He won't keep us guessing when it comes to our sin- He'll let us know. He has many ways of communicating to us about our sins and we should be open to however He wants to bring our conviction, and we should be quick to turn from our sin. We want to be like King David, who prayed, "Search me, O God, and know my heart; try me, and know my anxieties; and see if there is any wicked way in me, and lead me in the way everlasting.[13]

Conviction or Condemnation?

One of the things we can be thankful for in our lives is the conviction of the Holy Spirit. God guides and directs us, but He also rebukes and corrects us. As we are told, "All Scripture is given by inspiration of God, and is profitable for doctrine,

---

[11] Hebrews 12:5-11
[12] Psalm 119:67
[13] Psalm 139:23-24

for reproof, for correction, for instruction in righteousness."[14] However, there is a difference between conviction (reproof, correction and instruction in righteousness) and condemnation. God will convict us of sin- He will let us know that what we are thinking or doing (or not doing), or have done, is wrong.

the devil, on the other hand, doesn't convict us of sin- he condemns us. If you sense a still, small voice saying, "That is wrong," it could be the Lord. If the voice says, "You never do things right. You are weak, worthless, good for nothing...," it's probably the enemy of our souls. he loves to condemn us. he is called "the accuser of our brethren."[15] The word "devil" means "slanderer." It's who he is. he loves to make Christians feel badly, and to drive us away from God. God loves to restore us and bring us into a right relationship- to bring us closer to Himself. If the thoughts in your head are driving you away from God, there's a good chance they are just lies from the father of lies- the accuser. If the thoughts in your head are telling you things you need to do (or confess to God) in order to get right with God, you should listen. "There is therefore now no condemnation to those who are in Christ Jesus."[16] God doesn't want to condemn you- He loves you.

Learning from Love

There is so much we can learn from giants in the faith, people who have walked with the Lord for many years, people who have surrendered their lives to Him and who live lives that please Him. One of these people is the Apostle Paul. In the New Testament, Paul shares about some of the trials he went through, as well as his heart for the Lord. One of the most powerful statements of Paul in the entire New Testament is in the book of Philippians, which is a letter that Paul wrote from prison. There are two things that really stand

---

[14] 2 Timothy 3:16
[15] Revelation 12:10
[16] Romans 8:1

out as you read the book of Philippians, one is the suffering that Paul went through; the other is his joy.

As Paul sits in chains in prison for preaching the Gospel, he mentions that he doesn't know if he will live or die. And he can't decide between the two- he says, "with all boldness, as always, so now also Christ will be magnified in my body, whether by life or by death. For to me, to live is Christ, and to die is gain."[17] He says if he dies giving his life for the Philippians, "I am glad and rejoice"[18]

Paul is a man who began his relationship with Jesus, saying, "Who are you Lord?"[19] But who eventually got to the place where he could say, "I count all things to be loss in view of the surpassing value of knowing Christ Jesus my Lord."[20] Paul started out in the place of not knowing Jesus, but got to the place where all that mattered was knowing Jesus. Like Paul, the more we know the Lord, the more we'll love Him. And the more we love Him, the more we, like Paul will say, "Rejoice in the Lord always. Again I will say, rejoice!"[21] And we will say that even when we don't understand why something is happening the way it is. We can always choose to "rejoice in the Lord always."

> **Paul started out in the place of not knowing Jesus, but got to the place where all that mattered was knowing Jesus.**

Learning from Jesus

Jesus is of course, our greatest example. We are told that Jesus, "for the joy set before Him endured the cross, despising the shame, and has sat down at the right hand of the throne of God."[22] There are a number of things that are very significant

---

[17] Philippians 1:20-21
[18] Philippians 2:17
[19] Acts 9:5
[20] Philippians 3:8
[21] Philippians 4:4
[22] Hebrews 12:2

about that passage. Number one, Jesus endured incredible suffering- more suffering than you will ever have to go through. Secondly, He despised the shame. He wasn't saying, "Oh, Yippee, I get to suffer humiliation and torture." He hated what He endured. He "despised" it. And thirdly, He did it for the joy that was set before Him- the future joy.

You and I can have that same attitude when we face trials. Firstly, we can endure it by looking at Jesus and remembering that He endured the cross for us. He suffered far more than we ever will. Secondly, like Jesus, we may also hate what we have to endure sometimes. We shouldn't feel bad about that.

> "Therefore we do not lose heart... For our light affliction, which is but for a moment, is working for us a far more exceeding and eternal weight of glory."
> - 2 Corinthians 4;16-17

"There is a time to mourn."[23] Do you think Jesus was full of joy when he prayed in the garden on the night before He was betrayed and crucified? Was he happy when they were tearing the skin off his back and driving the nails in his hands and feet? No. It was a horrible experience. Thirdly, like Jesus, we can endure trials by reminding ourselves that great joy is in our future- unspeakable joy- joy that will make all of our suffering seem like nothing. Paul said, "Therefore we do not lose heart... For our light affliction, which is but for a moment, is working for us a far more exceeding and eternal weight of glory."[24] "For I consider that the sufferings of this present time are not worthy to be compared with the glory which shall be revealed in us."[25] And as Paul said, we are "sorrowful, yet always rejoicing."[26]

---

[23] Ecclesiastes 3:4

[24] 2 Corinthians 4:16-17

[25] Romans 8:18

[26] 2 Corinthians 6:10

Jesus is "God with us."[27] He has promised to take us to Heaven, and while we are on this earth, He has promised never to leave us. We are so quick to take our eyes off of Him however, and to be fixated on our situations. Jesus and His disciples were by the Sea of Galilee. "When evening had come, He said to them, 'Let us cross over to the other side.' Now when they had left the multitude, they took Him along in the boat as He was. And other little boats were also with Him. And a great windstorm arose, and the waves beat into the boat, so that it was already filling. But He was in the stern, asleep on a pillow. And they awoke Him and said to Him, 'Teacher, do You not care that we are perishing?' Then He arose and rebuked the wind, and said to the sea, 'Peace, be still!' And the wind ceased and there was a great calm. But He said to them, 'Why are you so fearful? How is it that you have no faith?'"[28]

Jesus and the disciples all got to the other side of the Sea of Galilee. Jesus arrived rested and at peace. The disciples arrived stressed out and exhausted, having just gone through an experience in which they thought they were going to die. But Jesus didn't say, "Let's go perish," He said, "Let's go to the other side." The disciples were terrified by the situation because they weren't focusing on Jesus and His Word. We are all going to get to the other side. God will be with us in whatever storms we encounter. We choose whether to be walking in faith- trusting in Him and His Word, or to be stressing out and saying, "Jesus, do You not care that we are perishing?" I don't want to go through this life, and get to the end of this life- stressed out and exhausted. I would much rather learn to trust in Him and walk in joy. Wouldn't you?

The Pit of Despair

I've been sick several times with life-threatening illnesses. I've had relationship problems. I've been betrayed. I've been

---

[27] Matthew 1:23
[28] Mark 4:35-40

broke and in debt, suffered from a broken heart, felt a tremendous burden of guilt, been lonely, lost close family members, been overwhelmed with fear and worry, and even considered suicide. I walked through some deep valleys before I received Jesus, but some of the deepest valleys I've gone through were after I received the Lord.

When I think of times in my life when I've felt the lowest, one particular period of time comes to mind. Why? Because what happened to me while I was in the valley was amazing.

It seems like it should have been a joyful time. I was serving full-time in a fruitful Christian ministry. I was (and still am) happily married. I was in good health. I had friends. I was part of a wonderful Christian fellowship. Doreen and I (along with the bank) owned a home. We had no debt other than our mortgage. I had a lot going for me, but I was in a deep valley. I felt like I was in the pit of despair. That phrase kept coming to mind, over and over- "the pit of despair." So why, when I had so much going for me, was I in a pit of despair?

I was serving in the Church Relations Department of the ministry. My job was to contact pastors and mission leaders in churches in the U.S. and let them know how their partnership was changing lives in previously unreached villages. (I also travelled to speak in churches around the U.S.). It was a blessing for me to talk with people on the phone. It was such a joy to talk with someone who is seeking to live their life for God, hoping they are making a difference in people's lives, and to help them realize they are a part of changing people's lives for eternity. I received a great amount of satisfaction from the conversations on the phone, as well as from being able to speak in churches and from hearing how the messages impacted people. To top it off, I worked alongside a wonderful bunch of people.

Then the drought came. Day after day, it seemed like there was no fruit coming from my work. I couldn't get a hold of pastors on the phone, and when I did, I didn't seem to be able to communicate effectively with them. Day after day, turned into week after week. It became depressing. I couldn't believe it- here I was, trying as hard as I could to produce results, and it seemed like all of my work was for nothing. I prayed hard. I worked hard- still no results. Why was I alive? Why was I pouring out my life? Why was I working so hard if it wasn't going to make a difference?

The "One-Step" Program

This may not seem like a very deep valley to you, but to me the idea of wasting my life was a serious issue- it hit me hard. I had nowhere to turn. I couldn't really get comfort from other people. As far as I knew, there was nothing I could do to change my situation. I had nowhere to turn- but up. So I did. I cried out to God, "God! What's wrong? What am I doing wrong? I'm working, I'm praying, but it seems like it's all for nothing." I cried out to God and grabbed tight. He was all I had. "God, You have to help me!" And He did. Did my life start bearing fruit again?

> Intimacy with God is the greatest thing we can seek in prayer. Everything else flows from that.

Not that I could tell (at least not at first). What happened was that as I cried out to God and poured out my heart to Him, He gave me peace and joy. I realized that I didn't really need to bear fruit- all I really needed was Him. There were actually two things about this valley experience that amazed me- one was that I was completely delivered from my pit of despair- even though I was still in the valley! The second amazing thing was how easy it was to find joy and peace in the valley- all I had to do was to draw close to God. I realized that my prayer times had for the most part, become times of seeking things from God, rather than times of seeking God Himself. Intimacy with God is the greatest thing we can seek in prayer. Everything else flows from that.

Drawing close to God in prayer and surrender was the answer. It was a "one-step" program. The solution to my problem was not at all what I thought it was- to bear fruit. I thought my greatest need was to get out of the valley- it wasn't. The solution was to draw close to God and find my joy in Him. Was it wrong to find joy in my work? No, but I had let work (even though it was serving God) become the main source of my joy. I was trying to find satisfaction in *something* instead of *Someone*. It felt like help was a million miles away. In fact, it felt like there was no way out. I had no hope of getting help to get out of my situation. The amazing thing about this valley was that help was right there with me all along. He was right there waiting for me. I just didn't realize it.

The psalmist writes, "I waited patiently for the LORD; and He inclined to me, and heard my cry. He also brought me up out of a horrible pit, out of the miry clay, and set my feet upon a rock, and established my steps. He has put a new song in my mouth- Praise to our God."[29] You may have felt that you were in "a horrible pit," a "pit of despair" at some point, or you may feel like you are in one now. You may think that your greatest need is to be out of the valley, to be out of the storm.

> God doesn't always deliver us from our valleys and storms when we want Him too, but He is always there with us in them. The key is to draw close to Him for strength and joy.

The Son is Shining Above the Clouds

Firefighters don't focus on how hot the flames are as they run into a burning house. They look forward; focusing on the goal of rescuing that child who is trapped in the house. And we can only run triumphantly into the flames, shadows and valleys of life with joy if we are looking forward; focusing on the Lord and the joy of Heaven. God doesn't always deliver us from our valleys and storms when we want Him too, but He is

---

[29] Psalm 40:1-3

always there with us in them. The key is to draw close to Him for strength and joy. God has a reason for allowing the storms in your life. And no matter what you go through in this life, "Weeping may endure for a night, but joy comes in the morning."[30] In the future, you will be able to look back and see why God is allowing you to go through the storm, but for now, I encourage you, cry out to Him, worship Him, praise Him, thank Him, trust Him and love Him. Cling to Him. He loves you and He is with you. When you feel like your life is a shipwreck and you are floating alone out on the high seas, you can rejoice like someone who's just gotten a cell phone call from the rescue ship. You can rejoice knowing that help is on the way. But even more, you can rejoice knowing that you have His presence and His promises. And Jesus promised, "I will never leave you."[31] Jesus is always with you.

Our Heavenly Father is the God who loves you so much that He sent His only Son to die for you. "For God so loved the world that He gave His only begotten Son..."[32] And to think that Jesus willingly chose to come to suffer for your sins, shows us how much He loves you. Jesus has been through a valley we can't imagine. He bore our sin, became a curse for us, was separated from

> **God knows why it is the absolute best thing to allow you to go through the fires, storms and valleys.**

God- not as a result of His sin (He was sinless), but as a result of His perfect obedience, and then He suffered the wrath of Almighty God. He has suffered more than any other human being ever has, and it was all for us. He wants to give you His peace and comfort. Cry out to Him. Cast all of your cares on Him- He cares for you. As you cast your cares on Him and pour out your heart to Him in prayer, He promises to give you peace.[33] He is your deliverer and He will help you. He may not

---

[30] Psalm 30:5

[31] Hebrews 13:5

[32] John 3:16; Romans 8:32

[33] Philippians 4:6-7

deliver you like you think He should, or when you think He should, but He knows everything and He knows why it is the absolute best thing to allow you to go through the fires, storms and valleys. And He knows when and how it is best to deliver you. One day very soon, He is going to come back to take you to Heaven. While you are in the valleys, He is with you- and He will never leave you. You have His promises and as you focus on your future joy, you will experience joy today.

"Why are you cast down, O my soul? And why are you disquieted within me? Hope in God; For I shall yet praise Him, the help of my countenance and my God."[34]

We can all live a life of joy, but there are things we do, sometimes on a regular basis, to sabotage our own joy. As we will see in the next chapter, sometimes we are our own worst enemy.

---------o----------------o----------------o---------

Father, Thank You for being on the throne. You are in control. Nothing happens to me or to those I care about, without it first passing through Your loving hand. You love me so much that You sent Your only begotten Son to suffer a horribly painful death for me. And Jesus, You came to pay the ultimate price so I can have the ultimate peace. I can trust You no matter what is going on in my life, no matter what has happened to me and no matter what will happen to me. Lord, You are faithful. You will never leave me nor forsake me. Help me to lean on You and trust You when I am going through the valleys, the storms and the fires of life. I surrender to You and am willing to let Your will be done in my life. Help me to take my eyes off of my trials and to put them on You and Your promises. Help me to be eagerly expecting Your returning to take me Home. Help me to focus on my future joy. I love You. In Your name I pray, Amen.

---

[34] Psalm 42:11

12

Joy Killers

"Restore to me the joy of Your salvation"
- Psalm 51:12

If you were sick with a debilitating illness that kept you in pain day after day, and a knowledgeable, trustworthy person told you they have the cure for your illness, would you take it?

For thousands of years, God had spoken to the Israelites through the prophets and yet they had (for the most part) refused to listen. Their hard hearts and stubbornness cost them greatly. As a result of the religious leaders' refusal to yield to God, they didn't even recognize their Savior- the Son of God who came to suffer for them, that they might have forgiveness of their sins, and that they might have joy.

As Jesus journeyed toward Jerusalem on His way to give His life as a sacrifice, He said, "O Jerusalem, Jerusalem, the one who kills the prophets and stones those who are sent to her! How often I wanted to gather your children together, as a hen gathers her chicks under her wings, but you were not willing!"[1] As a result of their hardness of heart, they missed out on unspeakable joy. We wonder how they could hear Jesus, how they could see the miracles He was performing, how they could see Him fulfilling so many prophecies about the Messiah, and yet not realize He was the One predicted by the prophets. Why didn't they know He was the One that came to bring them "great joy"?[2]

---

[1] Matthew 23:37
[2] Luke 2:10

Their hardness of heart kept them from receiving the great joy that was theirs for the taking. All they had to do was to soften their hearts in order to receive it. We can marvel at how they would be willing to miss out on something so good, simply because of their attitude. The truth is that sometimes our lives lack joy because of our attitudes as well.

> **It's possible for our lives to lack joy not just for a few minutes, hours or days- we can spend years needlessly suffering.**

In fact, it's possible for our lives to lack joy not just for a few minutes, hours or days- we can spend years needlessly suffering. I want to be one of those people who make choices that will lead to a life of joy. I don't want to suffer needlessly.

Sometimes, realizing we have gotten ourselves (or kept ourselves) in that place of suffering, anxiety or fear, is a huge first step on the road to peace and joy. There are a number of things we can look for in our lives; if we recognize them, and are willing to change our mind about them, we can move from a place of needless suffering, grief and fear, to a place of peace and joy.

Christianity at its core, is very simple. People sin. Sin separates us from God. Jesus came to reconcile people back to God. It's a simple truth, and yet it's so easy for us to walk or drift away from, or never fully enter into, the simple, intimate relationship with God that is available to every one of us.

Leaving Our First Love

We can be doing a lot of things right- we can go to church, try to do what God wants us to do (in fact we can be very "busy for God"), and even stay away from those things God wants us to stay away from, and yet we can be far away from God. As a result, we remain far away from His joy. In the book of Revelation, Jesus rebukes the church in Ephesus for leaving their "first love."[3] I have been guilty of this quite a few

---

[3] Revelation 2:4

times. Maybe you have been too. We go through the motions, the routine of our Christian lives, but our hearts are distant from God. We don't share our hearts with Him and don't seek to know what is really on His heart. Jesus says, "Remember therefore from where you have fallen; repent and do the first works."[4]

When two people fall in love, they spend a lot of time thinking about each other, talking to each other, expressing their love to one another, and sharing their hearts with one another. They can't seem to get enough of being with each other. That's what our relationship with the Lord should be like. As we will look at shortly, there are definite steps we can take- we can do those "first works," again, and we can have peace and joy.

Prayerlessness

To a large degree, we Christians (at least in the U.S.) live in a prayerless culture. According to surveys, American Christians spend five minutes a day in prayer (on average). We may wonder why we don't experience more joy in our lives, but if we are only spending five minutes a day interacting with God, we shouldn't really be wondering. We as Christians are the house of God- we are His temple.[5] Jesus rebuked those who were misusing God's temple in Jerusalem, saying, "It is written, 'My house shall be called a house of prayer,' but you have made it a 'den of thieves.'"[6] That rebuke is quoted three times in the New Testament.[7] As we looked at earlier, the phrase "house of prayer" is how God wants to be able to describe each one of us (and all of us together). He wants to make us "joyful" in His "house of prayer."[8] Would He describe you as a house of prayer? Is that how He would sum

---

[4] Revelation 2:5
[5] Ephesians 2:21-22
[6] Matthew 21:13
[7] Matthew 21:13; Mark 11:17; Luke 19:46
[8] Isaiah 56:7

up your life? Probably not- if you are only spending a few minutes a day in prayer.

I am not saying this to condemn you and make you feel like a bad Christian. My prayer is that every one of us would take prayer seriously- that we would cry out to God, "Please, Lord! I've lived too much of my life in my own strength. Help me to become a house of prayer!"

We are willing to make sacrifices for things we value. You see young people (and some not so young) standing in line for hours to get tickets to a concert. If you drive by a gym, you will see people paying the price to get (or stay) in physical shape. In the early morning hours, roadways in almost every city in the world are packed with cars as people pay the price to get to work to earn

> The phrase "house of prayer" is how God wants to be able to describe each one of us, and He wants to make us "joyful" in His "house of prayer."

money. Americans are willing to sit for almost five hours a day (on average) watching television, but we won't go to bed an hour earlier and set our alarm clocks to spend an hour with the Living God.

Paul said, "I discipline my body and bring it into subjection,"[9] and he said to "exercise yourself toward godliness."[10] We should "exercise" or "discipline"[11] ourselves toward godliness. With the Lord's help, we should bring our bodies into subjection for Him. We should put forth the effort to cultivate the discipline of prayer.

If people only knew what they were missing out on, every home in the world would have people awake in the early hours of the day, praying. If people knew what they were missing, they would often be telling their family members, "I'm sorry, I need to go to sleep now," in order to get up early so they can spend time with the Lord. There are so many

---

[9] 1 Corinthians 9:27

[10] 1 Timothy 4:7

[11] 1 Timothy 4:7 (NASB)

benefits of following Paul's admonition to, "Devote yourselves to prayer," that explaining them all would fill another book, but suffice it to say, if you aren't carving a significant amount of time out of your day to spend with God, you are really, really missing out.

God is committed to making us more like Jesus, Who, even after a busy day, "in the morning, having risen a long while before daylight, He went out and departed to a solitary place; and there He prayed."[12] Often times, I think God will give us a choice- either we choose to become people of prayer, or He will allow trials in our lives that will drive us to

> **If we are living lives in which intimacy with Him is not a priority, He may "turn up the heat" in our lives because He loves us.**

prayer. It's sort of like, "You can do this the easy way, or you can do this the hard way." He says, "Do not be like the horse or like the mule, which have no understanding, which must be harnessed with bit and bridle, else they will not come near you."[13] His desire is that we will come near to Him. He loves us and He knows what's good for us- and drawing near to Him is good for us. If we are living lives in which intimacy with Him is not a priority, He may "turn up the heat" in our lives because He loves us. If we won't come near to Him on our own, we will need to be "harnessed with bit and bridle." God wants us to learn "that men always ought to pray."[14] I wonder how many of us are missing out on the joy of the Lord because prayer is a passing thought and not a passion.

When talking with people about how wonderful it is to spend time in prayer with the Lord, a few people have said to me, "Well, I don't really have a daily time of prayer in the morning or evening, but I try to 'pray without ceasing,' throughout the day." It's great that people want to follow

---

[12] Mark 1:35
[13] Psalm 32:9
[14] Luke 18:1

Paul's admonition to "pray without ceasing,"[15] and I try to do that as well, but once I started making it a priority to spend time every day in prayer, my prayer times throughout the rest of the day were dramatically increased and improved. I'm sure Jesus prayed throughout the day, but He also got up a great while before day to pray.

God wants to give us joy- He wants to fill our lives with joy. But if we are neglecting a huge part of who we are supposed to be, it shouldn't be any wonder why we don't have more joy in our lives. Do you really desire to live a life filled with joy? Do you want to please God with your life? Is your desire strong enough for you to make some changes so that prayer becomes a priority in your life?

Wrong Priorities

Jesus warned about having wrong priorities. He said when God's Word is planted in people's hearts, some people's hearts are like thorny bushes- "Now these are the ones sown among thorns; they are the ones who hear the word, and the cares of this world, the deceitfulness of riches, and the desires for other things entering in choke the word, and it becomes unfruitful."[16] How many times have you heard or said, "I just don't have time to spend reading the Bible and praying every day. I have too much to do."

The Lord has convicted me of this sin. We get so busy and can come up with a hundred excuses. But do you want to get to the end of your life and find out that you have let "the cares of this world, the deceitfulness of riches, and the desires for other things" enter in to the extent that the Word of God has been unfruitful in your life? I don't.

You may have heard about the monkey trap- a hollowed out coconut with a hole drilled in it and tied to a stake, with something inside that monkeys like. A monkey reaches its hand in the hole to get the morsel but when it grabs a handful

---

[15] 1 Thessalonians 5:17
[16] Mark 4:18-19

of the goodies, its clenched fist is too big to pull back out of the hole. In its panic, the monkey doesn't let go of the morsel, and as a result is trapped.

Is it really worth it to let the things that will last for eternity fall to the wayside while you live for cares, deceitful riches and desires? No, it's not, but like Esau who traded his birthright, his whole inheritance, for a bowl of lentil stew,[17] we can squander our life and give up wonderful, eternal spiritual blessings, in exchange for a bowl of stew- all because we won't unclench our fist- we won't take our eyes off of what's right in front of us.

Eye Problems

It's amazing that the whole problem here is a matter of focus- what we are looking at. Are we looking at the cares of this world- all the routines of life that can take up all of our time, or the dark, foreboding valley walls and the raging surf and storm? Are we looking at the deceitful riches- the shiny trinkets and bobbles of this world? Are we focusing on the desires for other things, like the possessions, positions and praise that so many non-Christians live for? "If only I had that thing, or that person, or that stuff... If only I was over there... If only I was married... If only I was single..." Or are we fixing our eyes on Jesus and on Heaven?

The keys to victory in our lives are amazingly simple. We should be living our lives, running this race- continually "looking unto Jesus."[18] When the Apostle Peter was miraculously walking on water, he took his eyes off of Jesus, and started focusing on his circumstances and he began to sink. If we live our lives focusing on our circumstances, we will never know what it's like to miraculously walk on water- we will be people of little faith, and we will rarely experience His peace and joy- never knowing what it's like to live above

---

[17] Genesis 25:29-34
[18] Hebrews 12:2

the circumstances, being guided and strengthened by the Lord of miracles.

When we spend our time being troubled, it shows that we have lost our eternal perspective. Psalm 55:22 says "Cast your burden on the LORD, and He shall sustain you; He shall never permit the righteous to be moved." If we are being moved by every situation we encounter, it's a sure sign that we have lost our forward focus. We see Paul as he was heading toward "chains and tribulations," and even death, saying "But none of these things move me; nor do I count my life dear to myself, so that I may finish my race with joy..."[19] It's noteworthy that Paul said he wasn't moved by the coming trials, and secondly, he didn't count his life as "dear" to himself. It wasn't all about "Paul."

> **"But none of these things move me; nor do I count my life dear to myself, so that I may finish my race with joy..."**
> - Acts 20:24

We can easily lose our joy because our lives have become "dear" to us- we become precious in our own eyes. We value our lives too much.

Paul was passionate about finishing his race with joy, and he said, "and the ministry which I received from the Lord Jesus."[20] Paul was also passionate about finishing the work the Lord had for him. God has specific things that He wants to use us for. He wants to do great things through your life, but if you have "eye problems"- if your focus is off, you can miss out on those works that God has prepared especially for you. "For we are His workmanship, created in Christ Jesus for good works, which God prepared beforehand that we should walk in them."[21]

---

[19] Acts 20:24
[20] Acts 20:24
[21] Ephesians 2:10

I problems

Of course, if we have "eye problems," it's probably because we have "I problems." When the serpent tempted Eve in the Garden, he started his temptation by challenging God's Word, and then directed Eve's attention to what she could gain if she listened to the serpent's lie, "You will not surely die... Your eyes will be opened... You will be like God..."[22] Wow, it all sounded so good- all she had to do to find success was to start thinking of herself. She ate the fruit and gave it to Adam as well. He ate of it and then both Adam and Eve hid themselves from the God who loved them.

"Where are you?" God asked. Adam responded with excuses, "I... I... I... I..." He used the word "I" four times in one sentence. Yup, suddenly it was all about "I." And unfortunately, it's been pretty much that way ever since. Of course, it's not wrong to ever think of ourselves. We need to care for ourselves but the love of ourselves is something that comes naturally, and it can dominate our life. You hear people say things like, "Jesus said the second greatest commandment is 'You shall love your neighbor as yourself,' so we need to make sure we are loving ourselves first, before we can love others." But Jesus said that commandment is the "second" commandment, not the "second and third" commandment. Jesus wasn't telling us to love ourselves. He was telling us to love our neighbor. In giving us the command to love our neighbor, Jesus is telling us that we *already do* love ourselves, not that we need to start.

Selfishness

I love babies, but have you ever noticed what happens when they are old enough to learn the word, "mine"? They tend to use it a lot- it comes naturally. It's a trait they inherited from their father- Adam. And we don't grow out of

---

[22] Genesis 3:4-5

that trait very easily. Like the monkey with its fist stuck in the coconut, we keep thinking, "Mine!"

Of course, as we grow older, we become more subtle and sophisticated in our selfishness. We often don't recognize it in our selves. Praise the Lord, He's our deliverer. He offers a better way to go through life and He gives us the power to live it out. Jesus said, "For whoever desires to save his life will lose it, but whoever loses his life for My sake will save it."[23] As we seek to love others for the sake of the Lord, we will find great joy in life.

Pride

One of the ugly faces of selfishness is pride. You could say that pride is the root of all sin. We see lucifer's fall from Heaven after his prideful assertions, "I will... I will... I will... I will... I will..."[24] he was cast out of Heaven like lightning.[25] If only it was that easy for each of us to cast the pride out of our own hearts. We need to continue to choose to humble ourselves in this life. As Peter says, "Therefore humble yourselves under the mighty hand of God, that He may exalt you in due time."[26] Pride is a lot easier to see in others than it is to see in ourselves. For example, those of us who dislike receiving help from others, demonstrate in our self-sufficiency- pride. Those of us who struggle with anger, gossip or lust, demonstrate our real problem- pride. There are quite a few books written about how to overcome lust, but only a few of them deal with the real problem, the real dragon that needs to be slain- our pride. And the dragon of pride is slain one moment at a time, as we choose to humble ourselves and worship our God, and to walk intimately with Him, fixing our eyes on Jesus and Heaven.

---

[23] Luke 9:24
[24] Isaiah 14:13-14
[25] Luke 10:18
[26] 1 Peter 5:6

Fear

Fear has been a major problem in my life, especially as a child. There is a healthy kind of fear, as in "The fear of the LORD is the beginning of wisdom."[27] We should all have a healthy awe and reverence for God. But there are unhealthy fears as well- fears that keep us from what God wants for us. One of the most repeated commands in the Bible is "Fear not."[28] Apparently, I'm not the only one to struggle with fear. Fear is another display of our natural inclination toward selfishness and pride. And the devil wants us to focus on ourselves- whether that be in the form of puffing ourselves up or in fearing and fretting about ourselves. But if we know how much God loves us, we won't be prone to fear- "perfect love casts out fear."[29] God is on the Throne- He is in control, and He doesn't need you to fear and worry for Him. As Corrie ten Boom, who endured the Nazi concentration camps, says, "Worry does not empty tomorrow of its sorrow, it empties today of its strength."[30]

As Jesus said, "Which of you by worrying can add one cubit to his stature?"[31] Do you know of anyone who has added a foot and a half (one cubit) to

> **The solution to our fears is worshipful surrender.**

their height by worrying? Of course not. The idea is ridiculous and Jesus was illustrating that through His question. Worry doesn't do any good whatsoever.

The solution to our fears is worshipful surrender. When Esther was faced with the possibility of being killed for approaching the King in order to plead for the lives of the Jewish people, she was fearful.[32] Most likely, you and I would be fearful, too. Fear comes naturally to us, but when we

---

[27] Psalm 111:10

[28] Or other phrases with similar meanings, like "Do not be afraid."

[29] 1 John 4:18

[30] Corrie ten Boom, Clippings from My Notebook

[31] Matthew 6:27

[32] Esther 4:11

surrender to God and are willing to do His will, knowing that He loves us and that His plans are good, we can conquer our fears. We, like Esther, can say, "If I perish, I perish!"[33]

We can move forward, surrendering to God, saying, "Lord, I trust You. I know You are good and You are wise- You know everything. I know You are all-powerful. You are on the Throne in Heaven. I know I will be in Heaven with You soon. If I die, I die. I will go forward because You love me and I love You."

We can turn our fears into prayers[34] and through His strength, we can conquer them. God will give us courage to move forward, in spite of whatever fears we may have. As King David prayed, "From the end of the earth I will cry to You, when my heart is overwhelmed; lead me to the rock that is higher than I. For You have been a shelter for me, a strong tower from the enemy. I will abide in Your tabernacle forever; I will trust in the shelter of Your wings."[35]

People say that Jesus is just a "crutch" for us Christians. They are wrong. Jesus isn't just a crutch. He's the wheel chair, the life-support system, the hospital bed, the emergency room- He's the entire hospital! In fact, He's the Army, Navy, Air Force and Marines, too! What is there to fear? We are all going to die. Some of us will die living in fear, resisting God's will, and others of us will die in the center of God's will- worshipfully surrendered to walking with Him and doing His will. As a result, we will die in fullness of joy. As Paul said, "But none of these things move me; nor do I count my life dear to myself, so that I may finish my race with joy."[36]

> If you are trusting Him for eternity, you can trust Him for tomorrow.

The "prince of preachers," Charles Spurgeon said, "The cure for care (worry) is joy in the Lord. No, my brother, you

---

[33] Esther 4:16
[34] Philippians 4:6-7
[35] Psalm 61:2-4
[36] Acts 20:24

will not be able to keep on with your fretfulness; no, my sister, you will not be able to weary yourself any longer with your anxieties, if the Lord will but fill you with his joy."[37] Instead of asking God over and over to take your fears and worries, take your eyes off of yourself and focus on Him- start thanking Him for His help, and for His promises. He loves you and He is with you. You can go forward, "being confident of this very thing, that He who has begun a good work in you will complete it until the day of Jesus Christ"[38]

He is faithful! And if you are trusting Him for eternity, you can definitely trust Him for tomorrow. We don't know what the future holds but we know who holds the future. When you make that choice to surrender to God in trust, as you pray and surrender your life to Him, He will "fill you with all joy and peace in believing, that you may abound in hope by the power of the Holy Spirit."[39]

> **Instead of asking God over and over to take your fears and worries; take your eyes off of yourself and focus on Him- start thanking Him for His help and for His promises.**

Idolatry

The Apostle John knew and walked with Jesus Christ for many years and wrote the letter of 1st John near the end of his life. He wrote the letter with a purpose. He said, "these things we write to you that your joy may be full."[40] In our quest for joy, we definitely want to listen to what John has to say. The letter is written to Christians- John (and God) wants our joy to be full.

---

[37] A Sermon (No. 2405) Intended for Reading on Lord's-Day, March 24th, 1895, Delivered By C. H. SPURGEON,
At the Metropolitan Tabernacle, Newington On Lord's-day Evening, March 20th, 1887.
[38] Philippians 1:6
[39] Romans 15:13
[40] 1 John 1:4

He ends the letter with a sentence that might surprise a lot of people. He says, "Little children, keep yourselves from idols."[41] What? He's telling us Christians to keep ourselves from idols? Yes, he is. Here in the West, we may think it's strange to bow down in front of an idol to worship it. We might think that as Christians, this is one sin we won't be tempted by. Well, there may not be a lot of Christians bowing down to statues, but John's warning message, the last sentence of his letter, is a warning that we should pay very close attention to.

While you don't see many Christians in the West bowing down to statues; you see a lot of us staring at little glowing glass screens for hours every day, or driving our idols around, washing them every weekend and getting insurance for them, (or wishing we could drive them

> Anything other than God, that takes the number one spot in your heart- is an idol.

around, but not being able to afford them), or coming home from work, turning them on with a remote control, and bowing down for hours in front of them. (The average American watches about five hours a day of television!) Anything you devote yourself to, anything you think about all the time- anything (other than God) that takes the number one spot in your heart- is an idol.

I remember as a young boy, thinking all I needed to make me happy was a Porsche. I loved those cars. I thought about them a lot. I couldn't imagine a time when I wouldn't want a Porsche. In school, I would draw pictures of them as the teachers spoke. I knew which model I wanted. It seemed to me that it wasn't too much to ask- all I needed was a Porsche. For me, it was an idol. Paul says, "When I was a child, I spoke as a child, I understood as a child, I thought as a child; but when I became a man, I put away childish things."[42] I haven't

---

[41] 1 John 5:21
[42] 1 Corinthians 13:11

arrived but God has worked in my life and now, I have no desire to own a Porsche. I look back and think of how childish it was. My focus was steadfast toward having that one thing. Now my life is different. At least when it comes to expensive cars, "I put away childish things." There is so much more to life.

And as Scriptures tell us, "He who loves silver will not be satisfied with silver."[43] If you can't figure out why you don't have more satisfaction and joy in your life, you might want to ask the Lord to bring to mind anything in your life that has become too important- anything that has become an idol. "Their sorrows shall be multiplied who hasten after another god."[44]

Complaining

I read about a survey in which people revealed that (on average) they spend about 80 minutes every day being irritated or annoyed. They might not be complaining out loud for the entire hour and twenty minutes, but they are at least complaining in their minds. That's a long time especially in light of the fact that God says "Do all things without complaining..."[45] When you think about it, what (actually, Who) are all of our complaints ultimately against? God. When we complain, we in effect are saying that God either doesn't care enough about us, or isn't really powerful enough to make our situation different. (To inform someone that a situation is less than desirable is one thing, to complain about it is something else. We can usually tell if we are informing or complaining, by the tone that accompanies our "informing.")

Complaining is a huge joy (and faith) killer. If you spend some time thanking, praising and worshipping God, it will be difficult to start complaining afterwards. Conversely, if you spend some time complaining, you will find it difficult to

---

[43] Ecclesiastes 5:10
[44] Psalm 16:4
[45] Philippians 2:14

transition into a time of giving thanks, praise and worship to God. One activity is honoring God, the other is saying that He has created (or allowed) a world, or people, or situations, that aren't good enough. You have to admit- it doesn't sound right- "Lord, Thank You for saving me from Hell. Thank You that even though I was Your enemy, You have made me Your child. Thank You for giving me Your Spirit, but how could You let me get sick?" or "but I'm broke," or "but the car in front of me is driving slow," or "but the internet isn't working right tonight," or whatever. You can't find a place for complaining in this description of the fruit of the Spirit- "love, joy, peace, longsuffering, kindness, goodness, faithfulness, gentleness, self-control." When I die, I want people to want to write "He was faithful," on my tombstone, not "He was a whiner." If you want to be a person of great faith and great joy, it will be impossible until you take a stand against your complaining.

A Critical Spirit

Tied into complaining is another outworking of our pride-having a critical spirit. When we are prone to judging others, our lives will lack joy. Our sin nature wants to puff ourselves up by putting others down, so this is a trap we can easily fall into. Scripture says, "Who are you to judge another's servant? To his own master he stands or falls. Indeed, he will be made to stand, for God is able to make him stand,"[46] and, "Do not speak evil of one another, brethren. He who speaks evil of a brother and judges his brother, speaks evil of the law and judges the law... There is one Lawgiver, who is able to save and to destroy. Who are you to judge another?[47] Jesus said, "Judge not, that you be not judged. For with what judgment you judge, you will be judged; and with the measure you use, it will be measured back to you. And why do you look at the speck in your brother's eye, but do not consider the plank in your own eye? Or how can you say to your brother, 'Let me

---

[46] Romans 14:4
[47] James 4:11-12

remove the speck from your eye'; and look, a plank is in your own eye? Hypocrite! First remove the plank from your own eye, and then you will see clearly to remove the speck from your brother's eye."[48]

God wants us to come alongside people who are in sin, in order to restore them to Himself, not to look down on people, criticize them and gossip about them. Jesus said, "Moreover if your brother sins against you, go and tell him his fault between you and him alone."[49] "Brethren, if a man is overtaken in any trespass, you who are spiritual restore such a one in a spirit of gentleness, considering yourself lest you also be tempted. Bear one another's burdens, and so fulfill the law of Christ."[50] Bearing with one another and loving others,[51] rather than criticizing them, will honor the Lord and also brings us peace and joy.

Unforgiveness

Unforgiveness is a prison we put ourselves in. [52] We can carry bitterness with us for our entire lives if we don't make the choice (in certain situations, we have to make it repeatedly) to forgive. God forgives all of our sins even though we don't deserve it. Jesus said if we have been angry with someone without an absolutely good reason, we are guilty of murder. That's just one of the sins we are guilty of. Maybe the full number of sins we've been forgiven of adds up to hundreds of thousands or millions- but God has chosen to forgive us of every one of them. And He tells us we should be "forgiving one another, even as God in Christ forgave you."[53] That's a whole lot of forgiving. As we continually choose to

---

[48] Matthew 7:1-5
[49] Matthew 18:15
[50] Galatians 6:1-2
[51] Ephesians 4:2
[52] Matthew 18:21-35
[53] Ephesians 4:32

forgive and release others, we will be released and be free ourselves. Ask the Lord who you need to forgive.

Unbelief

The story of the how God led the Jews out of slavery in Egypt is amazing. He performed miracle after miracle, showing them who He is. From the plagues of Egypt, the parting of the Red Sea, the destruction of the Egyptian army, the pillar of cloud by day and the fire by night, to the miraculous provision of bread (manna) and quail in the wilderness- it must have been awesome. He showed them His love, His faithfulness and power, over and over again for 40 years. But in spite of all they had seen God do for them, most of the children of Israel were not able to enter into the promised land of blessings. Why? Because of their unbelief.[54]

We marvel at how anyone who had seen God do so much, could be in unbelief, but the unbelief came from their hardness of hearts.[55] Every one of us can harden our hearts

Never blame God for anything!

against God if we want to. We can easily come up with reasons why things should be different than they are- why God should do things differently. As a result, we too can miss out on the tremendous blessings God wants to give to us (and through us). Or we can choose to soften our hearts, to humble ourselves before God, to surrender, and to walk closely with Him- in peace and joy.

When John the Baptist was in prison while Jesus was out preaching the Gospel, John apparently started to harden his heart against Jesus. After all, John's mission in life had been to announce the coming of Jesus- preparing the way for Him. Now John was in prison for the cause of Christ and Jesus wasn't doing anything about it. Instead, "when Jesus heard that John had been put in prison, He departed to Galilee."[56]

---

[54] Hebrews 3:7-19
[55] Hebrews 3:15
[56] Matthew 4:12

John must have thought, "Jesus heard I got thrown in prison and He went to Galilee?!" John got angry at what Jesus had allowed him to go through. It seems that John hardened his heart and it resulted in unbelief- it caused him to lose sight of who Jesus is. John had been announcing to everyone, "Behold! The Lamb of God who takes away the sin of the world!"[57] Now he was sitting in prison, offended and blinded by his unbelief, asking, "Are You the Coming One, or do we look for another?"[58]

John probably wasn't blaming Jesus for his imprisonment, but he was blaming Jesus for allowing him to stay in prison. He must have been thinking, "He just leaves me here in prison and doesn't even try to get me out! Doesn't He care about me? Is He really who He says He is?" We can do the same thing John did. When things don't go the way we think they should, or we are in a trial of some kind, we blame God- either for causing our trial, or for not delivering us from it. We are offended at God. We harden our hearts and end up in unbelief- we become blinded and forget who God really is. We can be just like John.

Jesus said, "Go and tell John the things which you hear and see: The blind see and the lame walk; the lepers are cleansed and the deaf hear; the dead are raised up and the poor have the gospel preached to them. And blessed is he who is not offended because of Me."[59] Jesus reminded John of who He is, and then said, "blessed" or "happy" is he "who is not offended because of Me." If we want to be happy, we need to guard against the hardening of our hearts. Never take offense at God. Never blame God for anything!

Spiritual Warfare

It's very difficult to win a battle you don't know you are in.

---

[57] John 1:29
[58] Matthew 11:2
[59] Matthew 11:4-6

Imagine trying to walk down a path while there is an invisible person walking next to you, trying to push you off the path. It would help a lot just to know they are there trying to interfere with your walk. We may try to ignore the fact but the devil and his demons are real, and they hate our guts. Paul says, "For we do not wrestle against flesh and blood, but against principalities, against powers, against the rulers of the darkness of this age, against spiritual hosts of wickedness in the heavenly places."[60] We will be a lot better off, a lot sooner, if we realize that. In fact, realizing that the battle we fight is spiritual, is often 95% of winning the battle. God does not want us to be ignorant of satan's devices.[61]

As we seek to live lives that honor God, we will face opposition. Have you ever noticed that on days you go to church, there are more arguments in your family? Or that when you decide to do something for the Lord, sometimes obstacles seem to come out of nowhere? the devil put it on Peter's mind to tell the Lord not to go to the cross,[62] and his demons put thoughts in our minds as well. We need to take every thought captive to the obedience of Christ[63] by fighting with our spiritual weapons.

> **Realizing that the battle we fight is spiritual, is often 95% of winning the battle.**

In most cases, once we know we are in the fight, winning is easy. "For the weapons of our warfare are not carnal but mighty in God for pulling down strongholds, casting down arguments and every high thing that exalts itself against the knowledge of God, bringing every thought into captivity to the obedience of Christ,"[64] If we arm ourselves for the battle and fight, victory is ours. Our weapons are "mighty"- they are

---

[60] Ephesians 6:12
[61] 2 Corinthians 2:11
[62] Matthew 16:22
[63] 2 Corinthians 10:5
[64] 2 Corinthians 10:4-5

powerful. Our armor is truth, righteousness, the Gospel, faith, the knowledge of our salvation, the Word of God and prayer.[65]

While spiritual warfare isn't mentioned much in this book; by walking intimately with the Lord- as has been talked about in this book, we will be more sensitive to the enemy's attacks. he is an "accuser" and a "slanderer." A lot of his attacks are designed to steal our joy. Living lives of worship, praise and thanksgiving, standing on God's promises, and obedience to what we believe God wants us to do, goes a long way toward thwarting the enemy's attacks on us.

Notice that our weapons are mighty "in God."[66] That's why our weapons are so mighty- they are in God. In the Old Testament book of Second Chronicles, we are told about a time when the armies of three nations were all gathered together against the tribe of Judah, and against King Jehoshaphat, the king of Judah. King Jehosaphat and the people were in fear, and as they

> A lot of the enemy's attacks are designed to steal our joy.

cried out to the Lord, God said, "Thus says the LORD to you: 'Do not be afraid nor dismayed because of this great multitude, for the battle is not yours, but God's."[67] God then directed the people, saying, "Position yourselves, stand still and see the salvation of the LORD, who is with you, O Judah and Jerusalem!' Do not fear or be dismayed; tomorrow go out against them, for the LORD is with you."[68]

The people had to walk in obedience to what God told them to do, but the Lord is the One who gave them the victory. As God's people sang and praised the Lord, "the LORD set ambushes against the people of Ammon, Moab, and Mount Seir, who had come against Judah; and they were defeated."[69] The invading armies turned on each other and

---

[65] Ephesians 6:10-18
[66] 2 Corinthians 10:4
[67] 2 Chronicles 20:15
[68] 2 Chronicles 20:17
[69] 2 Chronicles 20:22

wiped each other out. God gave His people an amazing victory over a multitude that far outnumbered them, and the victory came without God's people having to lift one physical weapon.

Psalm 22:3 says "But You are holy, enthroned in the praises of Israel."[70] God "inhabits" or "dwells in" or is "enthroned" in the praises of His people. James tells us, "Draw near to God and He will draw near to you."[71] As we pray and choose to walk in obedience to God; as we trust Him, and love and praise Him- we will see amazing victories in our spiritual battles. If we're going to be in a battle (and we are), we want God in front of us, fighting the battle for us.

And as we will see in the next chapter, there are some very specific weapons that we have- weapons we can use to win in this great battle of life. We can fight the good fight and finish strong- strong and victorious- and full of joy.

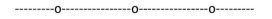

Heavenly Father, Thank You for being a loving God who wants to make me more like You. Thank You for pointing things out to me that I need to surrender to You. Help me to be open to change. Help me to listen to the conviction of Your Holy Spirit and to be quick to turn from sin in my life. Thank You for Your forgiveness. Help me to fix my eyes on You, Jesus, and on the things of eternity, and not on the cares of this world, the deceitfulness of riches, and the desires for other things that can so easily choke out the riches of Your Word in my life. Fill me with Your peace and joy. Whether You come back to take me to Heaven today, or years from now, help me to finish strong. May Your joy be my strength. I love You. In Your name I pray, Amen.

---

[70] Psalm 22:3
[71] James 4:8

13

The Way of Joy

"The joy of the Lord is your strength."

- Nehemiah 8:10

Just Another Day?

The day probably started pretty much like every other day for the past thirty-eight years. The sun rose and the man awoke from his sleep but couldn't get off of his bed. He couldn't stand up. He had been crippled for decades. Then a man spoke to him and asked him a question, "Do you want to be made well?"[1] The sick man must have thought, "Who is this man? Why would he ask a question like that?" The sick man explained to the man questioning him that his circumstances kept him from getting well. But Jesus wasn't asking him about his circumstances. He was asking him if he wanted to be made well.

Then Jesus told the sick man what to do. As soon as Jesus gave the man the command, he was healed. One of the reasons we like that story is because of the instant healing. The man had his infirmity for thirty-eight years and in an instant, he was healed. Wow! Jesus said, "Rise, take up your bed and walk,"[2] so the man did it. It's amazing.

Have you ever noticed that Jesus didn't just walk up to the man and say, "Rise, take up your bed and walk," or "Son, you are healed."? Instead, the first thing Jesus did was to ask him if he wanted to be healed. It was a valid question.

---

[1] John 5:6
[2] John 5:8

Sometimes when people are going through a trial, they get used to being there and they don't really want to be delivered. We can be stuck in a rut and for some reason, develop a sense of security in being there. We resist change, sometimes it could be fear of the unknown or we might enjoy feeling sorry for ourselves. But the sick man wanted to be healed.

Simple Steps

Elisha, a prophet of God, was in his house when Naaman, the commander of the Syrian army came to see him. Naaman had leprosy and had been told that the prophet Elisha in Israel could heal him. Naaman came with his horses and chariots and brought great riches to pay for the healing of his leprosy. As he stood at the door of Elisha's house, Elisha's servant came out and said, "Go and wash in the Jordan seven times, and your flesh shall be restored to you, and you shall be clean."

Naaman was furious, "'Indeed, I said to myself, "He will surely come out to me, and stand and call on the name of the LORD his God, and wave his hand over the place, and heal the leprosy." Are not the Abanah and the Pharpar, the rivers of Damascus, better than all the waters of Israel? Could I not wash in them and be clean?' So he turned and went away in a rage. And his servants came near and spoke to him, and said, 'My father, if the prophet had told you to do something great, would you not have done it? How much more then, when he says to you, "Wash, and be clean"'? So he went down and dipped seven times in the Jordan, according to the saying of the man of God; and his flesh was restored like the flesh of a little child, and he was clean."[3]

Naaman was insulted. He came to Israel to get healed by the prophet and was ready to pay a high price or maybe do some great deed in order to receive his healing. But God (through Elisha's servant) asked him to do something simple.

---

[3] 2 Kings 5:11-14

All he had to do was to humble himself, take a few simple steps, and receive what God wanted to give him. "Surely there's more to getting healed than that! Don't I need to jump through some great hoops or something?!" We can be just like Naaman.

Too Easy

We go through life thinking we need to do some great deeds or pay a great price, or wait a long, long time, in order to receive blessings and joy from God. We think only the "super godly people" can experience the fullness of His joy. And when the message comes to us that we can be set free from our ordinary lives, our depression, grief, worries, fear, monotony and boredom (and sometimes from the storm or valley as well), we don't receive the message- maybe because of the messenger- they aren't a prophet of God or anyone special, just another Christian- a servant of the Prophet. Or maybe it's because the answer to our problems sounds far too simple. "What? 'Just wash and be clean'? There definitely has to be more to it than that! I've been in this valley for a long time. How can it be that simple to find peace and joy?"

The truth is that God's grace is expensive, but Jesus has already paid the price for it. Now it's up to us to receive and walk in His grace- His undeserved kindness, His gift, His joy. God gives His grace to us freely- no charge. As we mentioned at the beginning of this book, the word "grace," in the New Testament, comes from the root word which means "to joy, rejoice, be glad." God's desire is that we would all have His grace, the fullness of His joy.

What if the lame man hadn't picked up his bed when Jesus commanded him too? What if Naaman wasn't willing to dip in the Jordan River seven times? Do you think they would have been healed? No, they needed to step out in obedience to what God was telling them to do. The healing, the deliverance, the joy, was theirs for the taking, but they needed to take simple steps (whether they sounded simple at the time or not). If we want to experience fullness of joy, we first need to consider the question Jesus asked the sick man, "Do you want to be made well?"[4] If the answer is yes, then there are some simple steps we can take to live a life of joy.

We mentioned earlier in this book that joy comes from abiding in Christ- we find joy in life to the degree to which we abide in Him. The closer we are to God, the more joy we will experience in our lives- "In His presence is fullness of joy."[5] Will we always be bubbling over like a kid in a candy store? No, but we will have an abiding peace and happiness that will, as Nehemiah says- be our strength.[6] Abiding in Christ- walking in that intimate love relationship with Him, gives us joy and peace that empowers us to be longsuffering, kind, good, faithful, gentle and self-controlled.[7] His joy gives us the strength to weather the storm, walk through the valley, to persevere through the fire, and to believe God for great things. His joy gives us the strength to be victorious in life.

Even when we go through valleys and storms, some of them deep and intense, we can still have God's joy and peace running through our lives like an underground river. We can be more than conquerors[8] as we go through whatever our loving God has allowed us to encounter, knowing that He is on the Throne and He will never leave us nor forsake us. However, how we face the storms and valleys makes all the difference in the world. Are we going to face them in our own strength, or in His strength? We can choose to do those simple, key things that will help us to abide in Christ and to live our lives in intimacy with our loving God.

---

[4] John 5:6
[5] Psalm 16:11
[6] Nehemiah 8:10
[7] Galatians 5:22
[8] Romans 8:35-37

The Way of Joy

These things may sound too simple, or you may not think I'm enough of an expert (I'm certainly not Elisha the Prophet) to be able to share them with you. I have probably never met you. The truth though, is that these are very simple things to do, they have been done by Christians for the past 2,000 years, we can all do them, and they will result in joy. Staying close to a person who we are in love with is easy- so is staying close to the God we are in love with. Just as investing in a human relationship will result in greater intimacy, investing in our relationship with God will ensure that joyful intimacy with Him that we desire. If we are willing to make these simple things an ongoing part of our lives, we will live the extraordinary lives God has for us. Here are the simple, but powerful steps we can take to have our lives transformed- to restore the joy we once had, or to rise to a place we've never been before- on the path God has for us- the way of joy. These steps are given in a simple acronym- R.E.J.O.I.C.E.-

R.- Read God's Word

It sounds too simple- "The statutes of the Lord are right, rejoicing the heart."[9] What? My heart will rejoice if I spend time in His "statutes" (His commandments, His direction)? Yes, like the promises in Psalm One- "Blessed (or "happy") is the man... (whose) delight is in the law of the LORD, and in His law he meditates day and night."[10] Many of God's truths sound too simple to be true- but they are true- every one of them. His statutes "rejoice the heart." We want our hearts to rejoice so we need to spend time prayerfully reading and thinking about His Word. As Jesus said, "Man shall not live by bread alone, but by every word that proceeds from the mouth of God."[11] Like food, we need to regularly take in His

---

[9] Psalm 19:8
[10] Psalm 1:1-2
[11] Matthew 4:4

Word. As Jeremiah said, "Your words were found, and I ate them, and Your word was to me the joy and rejoicing of my heart."[12] We've already looked at this earlier in this book, but this is a key to living a life of joy. If you want joy, spend time every day prayerfully reading the Bible (and seek to be obedient to what He tells you through it). Continually devote yourself to the Word.[13] It will lead to joy.

E.- Enter His Gates

Worship

The main thing is to keep the main thing, the main thing. As we've talked about in this book, we need to love God, first and foremost. Nothing is more important. Jesus said the greatest commandment is to "love the LORD your God with all your heart, with all your soul, and with all your mind."[14] And as the Apostle John tells us, "We love Him because He first loved us."[15] He is the initiator. We are the responders. God the Father loves you so much that He sent His Son to die for you. Jesus loves you so much that He came and suffered an incredibly painful death and shed His blood for you. Responding to God's love with your own love is the reasonable thing to do,[16] but it is also something you must choose to do on a daily basis.

We all fall short every day. Nobody is perfect, and we shouldn't feel condemned because we aren't living our lives as a 100% love offering to God, but our aim should be to live for God. The goal is to have everything we do be an act of worship to Him, in response to Him and His love. Paul said, "Therefore, whether you eat or drink, or whatever you do, do all to the glory of God."[17] Of course, a key to living this way is

---

[12] Jeremiah 15:16
[13] Acts 2:42
[14] Matthew 22:37
[15] 1 John 4:19
[16] Romans 12:1-2
[17] 1 Corinthians 10:31

to keep our focus on Him and Heaven, and not on ourselves and the things of this world. If we walk around thinking, "I'm going to love God. I'm going to love God," it won't last very long, but if we are fixing our minds on Him and on the sure hope of Heaven, the result is that we'll be walking around thinking, "I love You God. I love You God." Choosing to worship God in response to His love is a key to living a life of joy.

Prayer

Prayer is a key to knowing God, and to living a life of joy. Pray and ask the Lord how much time He wants you to spend in prayer every day. Listen for His answer. If you believe He puts an hour on your heart (or whatever amount of time it is), aim for that. Get serious about your prayer life. Go to bed early enough to help you to be able to get up early enough, and then spend time with Him, talking to Him, worshipping Him, thanking Him, praising Him, confessing your sins, praying for your life and for others you know, and people around the world (use news reports, world maps, etc.), and spend time listening to Him. Allow Him to guide you as you pray. Don't be in a rush just to get through a list. Spend time with God. He wants to be with you. Seek to listen to His "still small voice."[18] As the late Pastor Chuck Smith said to me about prayer, "What God has to say to me is a lot more important than what I have to say to God."

I wonder how many of the hardships in our lives are caused or allowed by God in order to get us to draw closer to Him in prayer. Please don't misunderstand me. I'm not saying that all of your trials are caused or allowed by God just to get you to draw closer to Him. But I am saying that because God loves us, He will use whatever is necessary to bring us closer to Him.

Even as Christians, we can easily live our lives as though God was at the other end of the universe. He is right here with

---

[18] 1 Kings 19:12

us and He wants us to fellowship with Him throughout the day, and in daily times set aside for prayer. In His presence is "fullness of joy."[19] As the psalmist writes, "Then I will go to the altar of God, to God my exceeding joy."[20] As we seek Him in prayer, He will be our "exceeding joy." We want to follow our Lord, who, even after a hard day's work, "in the morning, having risen a long while before daylight, He went out and departed to a solitary place; and there He prayed."[21] Follow Jesus- continually devote yourself to prayer,[22] and He will make you "joyful" in His "house of prayer."

Praise

We looked earlier at the ten lepers who were crying out, "Jesus, Master, have mercy on us!"[23] Jesus healed them all at the same time, but only one returned to "give glory to God."[24] We can marvel at the fact that nine of the ten men didn't even give glory to God, but how often do we neglect to give praise for Who He is, what He's done, what He is doing, and what He will do.

Praising the Lord is mentioned hundreds of times in the Bible. Over and over, we are commanded to praise the Lord. The fact that it is mentioned so many times tells us that it is important, and secondly, that it's something we need to choose to do. Psalm 148 starts with the command, "Praise the Lord!" It finishes with the command, "Praise the Lord!" In the first five verses of the psalm, there are nine commands to praise the Lord. In fact, the entire 14 verses of the psalm are either commands to praise the Lord, or reasons to praise Him.

In the longest chapter in the Bible (Psalm 119), the psalmist writes, "Seven times a day I praise You, because of

---

[19] Psalm 16:11

[20] Psalm 43:4

[21] Mark 1:35

[22] Acts 2:42

[23] Luke 17:13

[24] Luke 17:18

Your righteous judgments."25 Wow. The psalmist praises God seven times a day just for one of the many great things He does! The shortest chapter in the Bible has two verses and one message. It gets right to the point, and it's all about praise- "O praise the LORD, all ye nations: praise him, all ye people. For his merciful kindness is great toward us: and the truth of the LORD endureth for ever. Praise ye the LORD."26

Here are a few more verses in the Bible involving giving praise to the Lord- "I will praise Your name, for You have done wonderful things; Your counsels of old are faithfulness and truth."27 "Praise Him for His mighty acts; Praise Him according to His excellent greatness!"28 "I will praise the LORD according to His righteousness."29 "I will praise the LORD with my whole heart."30 "Praise the Lord... For His merciful kindness is great toward us, and the truth of the LORD endures forever."31 "Praise the LORD, for the LORD is good."32 "The LORD shall reign forever... Praise the Lord!"33 "The LORD is my strength and song, and He has become my salvation; He is my God, and I will praise Him."34

Praising God is not just something we should do when we feel like it. Praising God is something we choose to do. As the writer of Hebrews says, "let us continually offer the sacrifice of praise to God."35 Sometimes it's a sacrifice and we need to choose to make it a habit. We praise Him by declaring His goodness, His greatness, His majesty, His love, His grace, His mercy, His power, His faithfulness, and His mighty deeds, etc.

---

25 Psalm 119:164
26 Psalm 117 (KJV)
27 Isaiah 25:1
28 Psalm 150:2
29 Psalm 7:17
30 Psalm 111:1
31 Psalm 117:1-2
32 Psalm 135:3
33 Psalm 146:10
34 Exodus 15:2
35 Hebrews 13:15

Do you think we are commanded over and over to praise the Lord, simply because God wants to hear it? Is He egotistical? No. We are commanded to praise God because, in the first place, He is worthy of praise. He is worthy of "power and riches and wisdom, and strength and honor and glory and blessing!"[36] Praising God is the right thing to do. Secondly, it also benefits us to praise Him. Among the many benefits (like increasing our faith and love for Him and others), it results in joy. It's such a simple thing to do, and yet it can change your life.

Thanksgiving

In Luke Chapter 15,[37] Jesus tells the parable we commonly call "The prodigal son." He tells of the younger of two sons, who asked for his share of the family inheritance while his father was still living. (Since he was the younger son, he would get 1/3 of his father's wealth. The older son would get 2/3.) He took the money and wasted it on sinful living. The younger son then "came to his senses" or "came to himself" and realized that he was very blessed being his father's son. Even his father's servants ate better than he was now eating. He returned to his father and confessed his sin. His father received him with open arms and threw a big party to celebrate his son's return.

While there is a lot we can learn from the story about God's love toward us who don't deserve it, we don't want to miss a powerful truth in this parable- a truth about the older son- the ungrateful one. The older son, seeing how his father blessed his wasteful, sinful brother, complained to his father, "How come you never gave me anything? You haven't blessed me like you've blessed my brother."

How easy it is for us to fall into the same trap the older son fell into. "How come I'm not blessed like my brother is?" We see other Christians (or non-Christians) that have things

---

[36] Revelation 5:12
[37] Luke 15:11-32

we don't, whether they be relationships, material possessions, position, children, health, praise, or financial prosperity- and we complain because our Heavenly Father hasn't blessed us like He's blessed them.

We see the father's response to the older son. He said, "Son, you are always with me, and all that I have is yours."[38] Instead of being thankful for the blessings he had received, the older son looked at what he wasn't getting. We can be just like him. We can go through life thinking about why we should be blessed like other people are blessed. Like the older brother, we look for happiness in all the wrong places. "Son, you are always with me, and all that I have is yours."[39] God has given us eternal life. He allows us to know Him personally. He is going to take us to Heaven where we will be with Him in absolute fullness of joy forever. He has given us His Holy Spirit to be in us, with us, and to lead and comfort us. He has given us the Bible- the words of the Creator of the universe. He gives us every breath we breathe. He gives us the body of Christ- the church. The list of blessings He has given us and will give us, goes on and on. Whether it is through His presence, His promises, or His provision; God is the source of all true joy. We have an unending number of things to be thankful for.

It's no wonder God directs us over and over, to be thankful. We, like the older son, are so prone to a lack of thankfulness. Paul says, "In everything give thanks; for this is the will of God in Christ Jesus for you."[40] "In everything," is a whole lot of things- it's every single thing. Our lives should be filled with thankfulness. "Oh, give thanks to the LORD, for He is good! For His mercy endures forever."[41] As He says, "Son, you are always with me, and all that I have is yours."[42] Wow!

---

[38] Luke 15:31

[39] Luke 15:31

[40] 1 Thessalonians 5:18

[41] Psalm 106:1

[42] Luke 15:31

We have "God with us"[43] and possess "unfathomable riches."[44] If you want to live a life of joy, giving thanks is a habit you will want to develop.

Rejoicing

Jesus was "anointed with the oil of gladness."[45] He was a man who "rejoiced greatly in the Holy Spirit."[46] He tells us as His disciples, "rejoice because your names are written in heaven."[47] Rejoicing is not just an option for Christians; it's a command from God. No matter what is going on in your life, you can always "rejoice because your name is written in Heaven." Jesus even tells us to rejoice when we are persecuted. He says, "Rejoice in that day and leap for joy! For indeed your reward is great in heaven."[48]

Paul wrote, "Rejoice in the Lord always. Again I will say, rejoice!"[49] God had Paul say it twice in a row because He knows we need to hear it repeated. Notice that unlike the song writer who says, "Don't worry. Be happy," Paul didn't just say to rejoice. He said to rejoice in the Lord. We have a reason to rejoice and a source of power in our rejoicing- God Himself. Notice also the duration that Paul mentioned- "always." That's a lot of rejoicing. Who did God have speak those words? Paul, the Apostle who (as we looked at earlier) suffered tremendously and often faced the possibility of death.[50] If there is any Christian who has ever lived who might have reasons to complain about things, some would say it's Paul. Immediately after receiving the Lord, Jesus said "I will show him how many things he must suffer for My name's

---

[43] Matthew 1:23

[44] Ephesians 3:8 (NASB)

[45] Hebrews 1:9; Isaiah 53:3 tells us He was "a man of sorrows and acquainted with grief" but that is referring to His crucifixion, not His general disposition.

[46] Luke 10:21 (NASB)

[47] Luke 10:20

[48] Luke 6:23

[49] Philippians 4:4

[50] 2 Corinthians 11:23

sake."[51] Wow, what a way to start your Christian life! He endured a tremendous amount of suffering. Yet he said, "I am exceedingly joyful in all our tribulation."[52]

Psalm 37:4 says, "Delight yourself also in the LORD, and He shall give you the desires of your heart." The word "delight" is stronger than our English word for delight. A better translation would be, "Find exquisite joy." As we delight in Him and find joy in Him, He will give us desires, and He will satisfy those desires- He will give us what we want. Isn't that awesome? God will give you what you want if you delight and rejoice in Him.

In another letter, Paul says, "Rejoice always."[53] Choosing to rejoice in the Lord will result in thankfulness, praise and prayer. Praying (especially with praise and thankfulness) will result in us being closer to God. As we draw near to Him, He draws near to us. In His presence, there is fullness of joy. So when God tells us to rejoice and give thanks and praise, and to worship Him, it's not only because He is worthy of all glory, praise and honor, it's also because as we choose to rejoice, we will experience His joy.

J.- Jesus is Lord.

Jesus is God.[54] He is also the Word of God[55]- the expression of God to man. He is the only way to God[56] and He is at the center of our relationship with God. It's all about Jesus. He is the source of life, the source of hope, joy, peace, etc. He is, as the Apostle Thomas said, "My Lord and my God." It is therefore absolutely essential that we keep Him at the center of our lives. In order to live a life of joy, we must honor Him as our Lord and God.

---

[51] Acts 9:16
[52] 2 Corinthians 7:4
[53] 1 Thessalonians 5:16
[54] John 1:1
[55] John 1:1
[56] John 14:6

Obedience

As we looked at in the previous chapter; sin not only separates us from God, it separates us from the joy of the Lord. As we choose to walk in obedience to Him, there is a huge increase in our joy. "'There is no peace,' says the LORD, 'for the wicked.'"[57] Anyone who is not walking with God will not have His peace. As Hudson Taylor said, "The real secret of an unsatisfied life lies too often in an unsurrendered will. And yet how foolish, as well as how wrong, this is! Do we fancy that we are wiser than He? Or that our love for ourselves is more tender and strong than His? Or that we know ourselves better than He does? ... No wonder they are neither happy nor satisfied!"[58] While the "passing pleasures of sin"[59] may seem to satisfy us in the short term, they can't compare to the abiding peace and joy we get from a daily, close walk with Jesus (even if we are going through trials).

Jesus said if we want to find our lives, we need to lose them for His sake. Jesus is Lord- He is God and He is in charge. We need to allow Him to be in charge of our lives. "For the love of Christ compels us"[60]... "and He died for all, that those who live should live no longer for themselves, but for Him who died for them and rose again."[61] He died for us- we should live for Him. To the extent that we fight against that truth, we will not have His peace and joy. A lot of Christians live with discontentment in their lives because they are not surrendering their lives to the Lord. We are all "a work in progress" and we all fall short.[62] We shouldn't be living in condemnation, but we should be trying to walk in obedience to God. When we receive Jesus, we receive Him as Lord. That's who He is. He's not just "fire insurance" or a "buddy."

---

[57] Isaiah 48:22
[58] From Hudson Taylor, Union and Communion
[59] Hebrews 11:25
[60] 2 Corinthians 5:14
[61] 2 Corinthians 5:15
[62] Romans 3:23

He is the Living God who commands all men everywhere to repent and turn to Him as Lord.[63] And as the Bible tells us, surrendering to the God who loved us first, makes perfect sense.[64] As you surrender to Him, and to being who you were created and designed to be, you will find great joy.

Quick to Repent

It's amazing to me how we can spend hours, days, and even years, refusing to humble ourselves and turn from our sin and pride. We come up with all kinds of reasons why we harden our hearts- "But he... But she... But it... But God..." Or we can choose to humble ourselves- to die to ourselves and find peace and joy. Being quick to repent (change our mind) about our sin is a key to living a life of joy. We can be teachable or we can be like a mule that needs a metal bit in its mouth to be directed. Because He loves us and wants what's best for us, God wants us to come near to Him, and we can do it the easy way or the hard way. We all sin. We want to be quick to repent. We want to be like King David after he sinned, when he prayed, "Restore to me the joy of Your salvation."[65]

O.- Others

We were created to know and love God, and to glorify Him with our lives. It doesn't matter how hard a bird tries to become a fish- it will still be a bird. It may not be a very happy bird, but it will still be a bird. But if it surrenders to what it was created to be, it will thrive. And if we want to thrive, we should joyfully surrender to being who God has created us to be.

Love is at the core of the Christian life. It is at the core of God's will for our lives. "God is love,"[66] and as the Apostle John says, "Beloved, if God so loved us, we also ought to love

---

[63] Acts 17:30
[64] Romans 12:1
[65] Psalm 51:12
[66] 1 John 4:8

one another."[67] Loving God and people, especially Christians, is at the heart of what God created us for.[68] We will find a great amount of joy as we seek to love God, and to love our neighbors as ourselves, in whatever ways the Lord leads us to. Like the Sea of Galilee, we will overflow with life. "Abide in My love... that My joy may remain in you, and that your joy may be full."[69]

I.- Imminent Return of Christ

We have looked a lot in this book at the value of looking for our Lord's soon return. It is critical to living a life of joy. As we keep our focus on the soon fulfillment of His promise to return to get us, it will result in an eagerness in our lives. "For our citizenship is in heaven, from which we also eagerly wait for the Savior, the Lord Jesus Christ."[70] "We should be... looking for the blessed hope and glorious appearing of our great God and Savior Jesus Christ."[71] For truly, as He promised, "Surely I am coming quickly."[72] Be looking for His return. It could happen any second!

C.- Count it All Joy

"My brethren, count it all joy when you fall into various trials..."[73] We can make the choice to rejoice even in the trials of life. We can turn them upwards and do everything as unto the Lord. As Paul says, "Rejoice in the Lord always. Again I will say, rejoice!"[74] Even in the midst of suffering- "Though now you do not see Him, yet believing,

---

[67] 1 John 4:11
[68] Ephesians 2:10
[69] John 15:9, 11
[70] Philippians 3:20
[71] Titus 2:12-13
[72] Revelation 22:20
[73] James 1:2
[74] Philippians 4:4

you rejoice with joy inexpressible and full of glory."[75] Make the choice to rejoice- it will lead to joy.

E.- Encourage One Another

The writer of Hebrews says, "and let us consider how to stimulate one another to love and good deeds, not forsaking our own assembling together, as is the habit of some, but encouraging one another; and all the more as you see the day drawing near."[76] It is important for us to spend time with other Christians. Like logs burning in a fire, we need to stay close to each other in order to stay hot. If you take a burning log away from the fire, it will cool down and eventually become lukewarm. In the same way, we need each other to help keep us "stoked." We see that when God poured out His Spirit on the early church, "they were continually devoting themselves... to fellowship."[77]

Many Christians in the U.S. attend large churches but are not part of smaller fellowship groups. This makes it difficult to build relationships and to fellowship with one another. Of course, Biblical fellowship is not just getting together and talking about football or cooking- we need to share in the things of the Lord- spiritual things. The Bible doesn't just say we need to go to church, it says we need to fellowship, to share our lives with one another as Christians. Continually devote yourself to fellowship.[78] It will lead to joy.

The abundant life God wants to give us- the joy-filled life, comes from taking simple steps toward intimacy with God. If we are willing to take these simple steps to walk in the way of joy, we will find ourselves thinking about Him and Heaven a lot. We will find that we are preoccupied with the things of eternity, and the things of this world will lose a lot of their

---

[75] 1 Peter 1:8
[76] Hebrews 10:24-25 (NASB)
[77] Acts 2:42
[78] Acts 2:42

fascination to us. Instead of running this race staring at our feet, we will be looking to the finish line- and we will run well.

And now we arrive at the last chapter of this book, and we look to the end, and what a view it is!

---------o----------------o----------------o---------

Heavenly Father, I want the joy You want to give me- Your joy- fullness of joy. Thank You for making the way of joy simple. Help me to take those simple steps to have a daily, close walk with You. I want to know You more. You are Awesome! You are Holy! You are Perfect! And yet You want me to be close to You and to know You. It's mind- boggling that You, the Almighty God, would love me, that You would choose me before You made the world, to be Your child. I am in awe of Who You are. Please help me to draw near to You. Help me to train myself for the purpose of godliness.[79] Help me to be a person of Your Word, worship, praise, thanksgiving, rejoicing, obedience, quick repentance, love, expectancy, and fellowship- help me to walk in the way of joy. I love You. In Jesus' name I pray, Amen.

---

[79] 1 Timothy 4:7

14

What a View!

"We do not look at the things which are seen..."
- 2 Corinthians 4:18

Going Home

I sat on the edge of the bed. My grandmother, Nonie, was lying on the bed with the top half of her body in my arms. We were in her retirement home in Honolulu. Nonie was 92 years old and her health had been declining for several years. Two years earlier, I had explained to her about her need to be forgiven of her sins and about the promise of Heaven. I was blessed to pray with her as she had prayed to receive Jesus as her Lord and Savior.

For the last couple of hours, Nonie was not very comfortable. Her breathing was labored and she had some pain in her upper abdomen. However, the last ten minutes were peaceful. She breathed normally as she slept in my arms... and then she was gone. I felt a wave of peace come over me. I knew she was with the Lord. Her body was still in my arms, but Nonie wasn't. She was in Heaven. Her spirit had left her tent and she had "graduated." She was in His presence, in fullness of joy. She was Home.

You may have heard the story about the missionary couple returning to the United States from Africa in 1909. Henry Morrison and his wife had spent 40 years on the mission field, giving their lives in serving the Lord- bringing people to Christ and planting churches. They returned from Africa with no pension, little money, and failing health. They happened to be sailing on the same ship that U.S. President Theodore Roosevelt was on as he returned from a hunting trip in Africa.

As they arrived in the port in New York City, Henry and his wife saw thousands of cheering people at the dock. They were all there to greet the President. The Mayor and other dignitaries were there. Banners were waving that said, "Welcome Home." Even a marching band was playing for President Roosevelt. Nobody was at the dock to greet Henry and his wife. They checked into a cheap apartment in the city. Henry was broken hearted. He broke down crying and poured his heart out to the Lord in prayer- President Roosevelt had gone on a one week vacation and thousands of people were waiting to greet him when he got home. The Morrisons had spent 40 years pouring out their lives in Africa and not a single person was at the dock to welcome them home. As he cried out to the Lord, Henry felt the Lord speak to his heart, "But Henry, you're not home yet."

A Crown

In his last recorded letter, written shortly before he was killed for his faith, the Apostle Paul wrote, "For I am already being poured out as a drink offering, and the time of my departure is at hand. I have fought the good fight, I have finished the race, I have kept the faith. Finally, there is laid up for me the crown of righteousness, which the Lord, the righteous Judge, will give to me on that Day, and not to me only but also to all who have loved His appearing."[1] Paul knew he wasn't Home yet, but that Home was very close.

Paul may be the greatest Christian who ever lived. It's no wonder he looked forward to receiving the "crown of righteousness" when he got to Heaven. Paul was "poured out as a drink offering" for the Lord. He "fought the good fight," "finished the race" and "kept the faith." It's no wonder he was

---

[1] 2 Timothy 4:6-8

so excited about going to Heaven- great rewards awaited him. But wait, did you notice the "and not only to me" part of his claim? He said he wasn't the only one who gets awarded the "crown of righteousness." It is also awarded to "all who have loved His appearing." Isn't that great? That's us! That's all of us who have put our trust in Jesus and are looking forward to His return.

As you read through verses in the Bible that talk about the Christian faith; what Heaven will be like, what our attitude toward life should be, and what our focus should be on, you can't help but get excited. Over and over and over, we are told about the future focus of the faith that saves us- "without faith it is impossible to please Him, for he who comes to God must believe that He is, and that He is a rewarder..."[2] A critical aspect of our faith is that future focus- we believe God "is a rewarder." As we take those simple steps to keep our focus on Jesus and on our future Home, as we "diligently seek Him,"[3] we find that our lives are radically transformed. His joy becomes our joy, and His joy becomes our strength.

We "do not look at the things which are seen, but at the things which are not seen. For the things which are seen are temporary, but the things which are not seen are eternal."[4] We realize that "our light affliction, which is but for a moment, is working for us a far more exceeding and eternal weight of glory."[5] Heaven is going to be so much better than anything we can imagine. "The sufferings of this present time are not worthy to be compared with the glory which shall be revealed in us."[6] What may in this life seem overwhelming, will shortly be clearly seen as what it really is- momentary "light affliction." For all of eternity we will be able to say, "God, Your ways are perfect." We will understand what we

---

[2] Hebrews 11:6
[3] Hebrews 11:6
[4] 2 Corinthians 4:18
[5] 2Corinthians 4:17
[6] Romans 8:18

don't now. We will see clearly and say, "Thank You, God- You allowed me to be a part of Your great and wonderful plan."

At times Heaven may seem like a distant reality, but we know it's really just a few more breaths away- a few more heartbeats and we'll be there- in joy beyond our wildest dreams. "For what is your life? It is even a vapor that appears for a little time and then vanishes away."[7] Like a puff of smoke rising from a flame, our lives are here for a moment, and then we are gone- to a better place. As John Calvin said, "Let us consider this settled, that no one has made progress in the school of Christ who does not joyfully await the day of death and final resurrection."[8]

There is an old saying, "That person is so heavenly minded, they are no earthly good." That saying isn't really true. As C. S. Lewis wrote, "If you read history you will find that the Christians who did most for the present world were just those who thought most of the next. The Apostles themselves, who set on foot the conversion of the Roman Empire, the great men who built up the Middle Ages, the English Evangelicals who abolished the Slave Trade, all left their mark on Earth, precisely because their minds were occupied with Heaven."[9] Looking to our future joy is not a distraction from living life to the fullest; it's the key to living life to the fullest.

> **Looking to our future joy is not a distraction from living life to the fullest; it's the key to living life to the fullest.**

The Joy Revolution

Jesus was a revolutionary. He came to totally change how people live and how we see life. He came to start a revolution of happiness and joy. And that's not just my opinion- let's look at a little of the Biblical evidence for that claim. The

---

[7] James 4:14
[8] John Calvin, Institutes, 3.10.5.
[9] C.S. Lewis, Mere Christianity (San Francisco: HarperSanFrancisco, Harper edition, 2001), pp. 134-135

announcement of Jesus' birth was "good news of great joy."[10] The news of His entry into Jerusalem was a reason for people to "rejoice greatly."[11] Jesus came to suffer and die for our sins, and to rise again from the dead on the third day. That's the Gospel[12]- the "good news of happiness."[13] He gives us the joy of His salvation.[14] As we walk with Jesus and trust in Him, we will be happy- "whoever trusts in the LORD, happy is he."[15] As we believe in Him, we can rejoice with "inexpressible" joy.[16] As we abide in Jesus, His joy will remain in us and our joy will be full.[17] As we spend time in His presence, we experience "fullness of joy."[18] He tells us to pray; so that our "joy may be full."[19] We can serve the Lord "with joy and gladness of heart."[20] We are blessed to be able to share His "good news of happiness"[21] with others.[22] He gives us the fruit of joy in our lives.[23] The joy of the Lord is our strength.[24] He gives us the joy of fellowship with God and other Christians.[25] He came to bring us the Kingdom of God- so we can live in righteousness, peace and joy.[26] He gives us the joy of making disciples.[27] He gives us the joy of loving others.[28]

---

[10] Luke 2:10
[11] Zechariah 9:9
[12] 1 Corinthians 15:1-4
[13] Isaiah 52:7 (NASB)
[14] Psalm 51:12
[15] Proverbs 16:20
[16] 1 Peter 1:8
[17] John 15:11
[18] Psalm 16:11
[19] John 16:24
[20] Deuteronomy 28:47
[21] Isaiah 52:7 (NASB)
[22] Mark 16:15
[23] John 14:16-17; Galatians 5:22
[24] Nehemiah 8:10
[25] 1 John 1:3-4
[26] Romans 14:17
[27] 1 Thessalonians 2:19-20; Philippians 4:1; 3 John 1:4; 2 Corinthians 1:24
[28] John 15:9,11

He has given us the Bible- His Word, and as Jeremiah said, "Your word was to me the joy and rejoicing of my heart."[29] He gives us the ability to be "exceedingly joyful in all our tribulation."[30] Because of Jesus, we know that "weeping may endure for a night, but joy comes in the morning."[31] He said, "rejoice because your names are written in heaven."[32] If we are persecuted, He says, "rejoice in that day and leap for joy."[33] Jesus came to bring "great joy which will be to all people."[34] When we are all gathered in His presence, we will "shout aloud for joy."[35] We will enter His joy[36] and spend the rest of eternity in Heaven- in fullness of joy.[37] To sum it up- Jesus came to give us grace and mercy- God's undeserved kindness- that which results in joy. Jesus came to radically change our lives- Jesus came to start a joy revolution.

Looking Toward the City

Jesus said, "rejoice because your names are written in heaven."[38] We looked earlier at the "Great Hall of Faith" in Hebrews Chapter 11. It is very inspiring to look at the lives of some of the believers who have gone before us- people who accomplished great escapes, great endeavors and great endurances for God. As Hebrews tells us, they were all looking to their future joy in Heaven. You can't help but be in awe of their faith. We are told, "These all died in faith, not having received the promises, but having seen them afar off were assured of them, embraced them and confessed that they were

---

[29] Jeremiah 15:16
[30] 2 Corinthians 7:4; James 1:2
[31] Psalm 30:5
[32] Luke 10:20
[33] Luke 6:23
[34] Luke 2:10 (NASB)
[35] Psalm 132:16
[36] Matthew 25:21
[37] Psalm 16:11
[38] Luke 10:20

strangers and pilgrims on the earth. For those who say such things declare plainly that they seek a homeland... But now they desire a better, that is, a heavenly country... for He has prepared a city for them."[39]

Great Escapes

These believers were able to accomplish great escapes from temptation. Take Moses for example, who could have become incredibly wealthy. He was raised as the adopted son of Pharaoh's daughter. Moses could have lived his entire life in splendor, enjoying the amazing riches of Egypt. He forsook it all and chose instead to risk being killed, because "he looked to the reward."[40] Unlike Esau, who sold his future inheritance for a bowl of stew, Moses chose the eternal over the immediate. In the United States, it is so easy to get caught up in living for the things of this world and the deceitfulness of riches- the bowl of stew; we would be wise to learn from Moses' future focus. His focus on the future reward was the key to his strength- the key to his great escape from temptation.

Great Endeavors

Secondly, the future focus of our faith is also a key to accomplishing great endeavors in life. We see that those who were embracing that future city, the Heavenly city "through faith subdued kingdoms, worked righteousness, obtained promises, stopped the mouths of lions, quenched the violence of fire, escaped the edge of the sword, out of weakness were made strong, became valiant in battle, turned to flight the armies of the aliens. Women received their dead raised to life again."[41] That's amazing! All those miracles! How did they do it? The writer of Hebrews says it was by looking to the future-

---

[39] Hebrews 11:13-14, 16
[40] Hebrews 11:26
[41] Hebrews 11:33-35

it was by their "assurance of things hoped for, the conviction of things not seen."[42]

Great Endurances

Thirdly, having a future focus enables us to have great endurance- to go through the fires, storms and valleys. Again, in Hebrews Chapter 11, we see that "others were tortured, not accepting deliverance, that they might obtain a better resurrection. Still others had trial of mockings and scourgings, yes, and of chains and imprisonment. They were stoned, they were sawn in two, were tempted, were slain with the sword. They wandered about in sheepskins and goatskins, being destitute, afflicted, tormented- of whom the world was not worthy. They wandered in deserts and mountains, in dens and caves of the earth."[43] How could they do it? Like Abraham, who "went out, not knowing where he was going,"[44] they walked by faith, waiting "for the city which has foundations, whose builder and maker is God."[45]

Are we going to live our lives as people who are slogging through the mud, or as people who realize that we are campers, whose eyes are fixed on the prize, "the joy that is set before us"[46]- Jesus and the glory of Heaven? Will we be people who wake up every day and think, "Oh, well. It's just another day. Same old, same old world." Or will we be people who are eagerly expecting the return of Christ, people who know that He could come back any moment to take us home. Will we be people who accomplish great escapes, great endeavors and great endurances for God- will we be people of joy? We make the choice every day. Are we focusing on the things of this world or are we taking the simple steps to keep our focus on Jesus?

---

[42] Hebrews 11:1
[43] Hebrews 11:35-38
[44] Hebrews 11:8
[45] Hebrews 11:10
[46] Hebrews 12:2

Just as Jesus promised, there are trials in our lives.[47] Sometimes the fires, storms and valleys are more than we can handle, but He is with us, and He will continue to be with us. The Son is always shining above the clouds. We can face any trial, knowing that the One who suffered more than anyone else ever has, is with us in our trials. And we can take comfort knowing that He who endured the cross and is now seated at the right hand of the Throne of God in Heaven, is also caring for us at every moment. We don't grieve and fear like the unbelievers who have no hope. We have two things that make all the difference in the world- God's presence and God's promises.

> **Will we be people who accomplish great escapes, great endeavors and great endurances for God- will we be people of joy? We make the choice every day.**

And our lives should look radically different than their lives. We have Him and we have hope! He said, "Behold, I am with you always, even to the end of the age,"[48] and He said, "I go and prepare a place for you... I will come again and receive you to Myself; that where I am, there you may be also."[49]

We press on, knowing that God is faithful. He works all things together for our good[50] and He is for us.[51] He will finish the work He began in each one of us.[52] As we fix our eyes on Him and on Heaven, He will make us more and more like Himself,[53] He will give us His joy, and then He will take us to Heaven. For now, we walk with Him and we look forward in hope- in desire and expectation, wanting and waiting for the wonderful things God has in store for us. And it brings us joy- the joy that comes from the good news from a country we

---

[47] John 16:33

[48] Matthew 28:20

[49] John 14:2-3

[50] Romans 8:28

[51] Romans 8:31

[52] Philippians 1:6

[53] 2 Corinthians 3:18

have not yet visited, but have seen from a distance, a country that cannot be adequately described by words- a country that is wonderful beyond our wildest dreams, hopes or imagination. We have a hope that keeps us going even when everything else is failing around us, because it is a hope worth rejoicing in-[54] it is a sure hope, and it is a wonderful hope.

Happy or Holy?

Sometimes you will hear people say, "God doesn't want you to be happy. He wants you to be holy." Their point is that God is the most important person in the universe- you aren't. And God wants to make us holy (set apart for Him). That's far more important than whether we are feeling happy at any given moment. However, the truth is that holiness and happiness aren't two opposite choices. In fact, they are connected. As a general rule- if you are holy; you will be happy. As Jonathan Edwards said, "God's purpose for my life was that I have a passion for God's glory and that I have a passion for my joy in that glory, and that these two are one passion."

But don't just take Jonathan Edwards' and my word for it. Jesus said, "Abide in Me, and I in you... These things I have spoken to you, that My joy may remain in you, and that your joy may be full.[55] As we pursue holiness- "Abide in Me," He will give us happiness- "that your joy may be full." As we take those simple steps to keep our eyes on Him and seek to walk with Him, we will walk in "righteousness, peace and joy."[56] God wants us to be holy and happy.

> "God's purpose for my life was that I have a passion for God's glory and that I have a passion for my joy in that glory, and that these two are one passion."
> - Jonathan Edwards

---

[54] Romans 12:12
[55] John 15:4, 11
[56] Romans 14:17

People may ridicule you. You will be persecuted- "Yes, and all who desire to live godly in Christ Jesus will suffer persecution."[57] You may lose family members and jobs and possessions. You may not have a place to live or food to eat. You may have your head chopped off for your faith. You may be tortured to death, but you can be happy. Because Biblical "happiness"- true joy, does not come from our situations, it comes from our God.

As Christians, we are people who belong to the Kingdom of God, the Kingdom of Heaven. Jesus described the Kingdom of Heaven in terms of the most joyous occasion that people He was talking to could understand- He compared it to a wedding feast.[58] God wants you to be filled with joy, not a joy that comes because you have riches, fame or comfort, but a joy that comes from your relationship with Him.

> Jesus described the Kingdom of Heaven in terms of the most joyous occasion that people He was talking to could understand- He compared it to a wedding feast.

As we aim for holiness; happiness will be a result. Will we always be bubbling over with happiness? No. In this life, we will have tribulation, and there is a time to grieve, but we can take heart, Jesus has overcome the world.[59] God should be the true north on our compass. In Him is found everything we need. Our focus must be on Him. And if it is, we will find a joy that can't be found anywhere else on earth, a joy that is our strength- a joy that gives us the ability to accomplish great escapes, great endeavors and great endurances for God.

Joy is definitely not a side issue in our Christian life; it is at the core of what God wants to give us. God doesn't want us to get through this life as mere survivors; He wants us to be "more than conquerors." "For the kingdom of God is...

---

[57] 2 Timothy 3:12
[58] Matthew 22:2, 4
[59] John 16:33

righteousness and peace and joy in the Holy Spirit."[60] God wants us to face life with wind in our sails- the wind of His Spirit. We shouldn't feel guilty or fearful because we want to live a life of joy- God desires that every one of us live in the fullness of joy. God wants to give us His joy- a joy that can't be found in the passing pleasures of sin, or the temporary thrills of the pursuits of this world. He wants us to have a joy that will make non-Christians jealous, a joy that is so rich; it can't be put into words- a joy that is "inexpressible." He wants us to have a joy that will help us accomplish things that others think are impossible, endure things we never thought we could, and to finish strong- very strong. He wants us to keep our eyes on the prize and like the Apostle Paul- to say, "that I may finish my race with joy."[61]

God doesn't want you to trudge across the finish line of life; He wants you to fly across it with the wings of faith on the winds of joy. God wants to do amazing things in and through your life, not because you are an amazing person, but because He is the amazing God. He is the same yesterday, today and forever.[62] He is the God who created the universe when no universe existed. He is the God who raised Jesus from the dead. He is the God who is working in and through your life for His glory and who wants to do even more. And He is the God who loves you. He is the source of all true joy. And He is the God who wants to fill you with His joy. Be a revolutionary- "Rejoice in the Lord always. Again I will say, rejoice!"[63]

The prophet Isaiah tells us, "You will keep him in perfect peace, whose mind is stayed on You, because he trusts in You."[64] "Perfect peace" is God's promise. We all want perfect peace, and God promises to give it to us if we do our part- keep our minds fixed on Him. We've talked in this book about

---

[60] Romans 14:17
[61] Acts 20:24
[62] Hebrews 13:8
[63] Philippians 4:4
[64] Isaiah 26:3

how to do that. Does it sound too easy? Try it; you'll find yourself living a life of joy.

"Though now you do not see Him, yet believing, you rejoice with joy inexpressible and full of glory." - 1 Peter 1:8

"But if we hope for what we do not see, we eagerly wait for it with perseverance."   - Romans 8:25

"Whoever trusts in the LORD, happy is he."
                                                   - Proverbs 16:20

"But those who wait on the LORD shall renew their strength; they shall mount up with wings like eagles, they shall run and not be weary, they shall walk and not faint."
                                                   - Isaiah 40:31

"The kingdom of God is... righteousness and peace and joy in the Holy Spirit."   - Romans 14:17

"Abide in Me, and I in you... These things I have spoken to you, that My joy may remain in you, and that your joy may be full.[1]   - John 15:4, 11

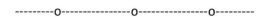

Heavenly Father, Thank You for being such an awesome God. Thank You for giving me eternal life. Thank You for Your presence, Your promises, and Your provision. Thank You that the best experiences in this world are just a taste of what is to come. Thank You for loving me with an everlasting love. Jesus, Thank You for suffering and dying for me and for going to prepare a place for me in Heaven. I know I'm just a camper here and You could come back any second to take me Home. Help me to be eagerly expecting

---

[1] John 15:4, 11

You to come to take me to Heaven. Help me to abide in faith, hope and love- help me to abide in You. Help me to fix my eyes on You, Jesus, who for the joy set before You, endured the cross and have sat down at the right hand of the throne of God. Fill me with Your joy. Thank You for Your joy. Maranatha! Come quickly, Lord Jesus. In Your name I pray, Amen.

God bless you as you walk with Him in joy.

If you'd like a free Study Guide, or to order copies of *The Place of Joy*, or my other book, *How to Know the Will of God*, check out:

www.firstcallpublishing.org

or call- (toll free) (800) 456-2421

If you were blessed by this book, I'd love to hear it. You can email me at: **strat@firstcallpublishing.org**

(And please consider leaving a positive review on amazon.com and/or bn.com)

Keys to Joy- R.E.J.O.I.C.E.-

R.- Read God's Word.

"Man shall not live by bread alone, but by every word that proceeds from the mouth of God." - Matthew 4:4

"Your word was to me the joy and rejoicing of my heart."
- Jeremiah 15:16

"If you abide in Me, and My words abide in you... that My joy may remain in you, and that your joy may be full."
- John 15:7,11

E.- Enter His gates.

-Worship, Prayer, Praise, Thanksgiving, and Rejoicing

"Oh come, let us worship and bow down; Let us kneel before the LORD our Maker. For He *is* our God..."
- Psalm 95:6-7

"I will... make them joyful in My house of prayer."
- Isaiah 56:7

"Praise the LORD, all nations... For His lovingkindness is great toward us, and the truth of the LORD is everlasting. Praise the LORD!" - Psalm 117:1-2

"Enter into His gates with thanksgiving, and into His courts with praise. Be thankful to Him, and bless His name." - Psalm 100:4

"Rejoice always, pray without ceasing, in everything give thanks; for this is the will of God in Christ Jesus for you."
- 1 Thessalonians 5:16-18

J.- Jesus is Lord.

-Obey Him and be quick to repent.

"At the name of Jesus every knee should bow, of those in heaven, and of those on earth, and of those under the earth, and that every tongue should confess that Jesus Christ *is* Lord." - Philippians 2:10-11

"Fixing our eyes on Jesus, the author and perfecter of faith, who for the joy set before Him endured the cross, despising the shame, and has sat down at the right hand of the throne of God." - Hebrews 12:2

1- Think about Jesus often.

2- Think about what Jesus did for you. (You are the joy that was set before Him.)

3- Think about the fact that He's in Heaven and could come to take you to Heaven at any moment.

O.- Others.

"Abide in My love... that My joy may remain in you, and that your joy may be full." - John 15:9, 11

"A new commandment I give to you, that you love one another; as I have loved you, that you also love one another." - John 13:34

"As we have opportunity, let us do good to all, especially to those who are of the household of faith."
- Galatians 6:10

"Therefore, my beloved brethren, be steadfast, immovable, always abounding in the work of the Lord, knowing that your labor is not in vain in the Lord."
- 1 Corinthians 15:58

I.- Imminent return of Christ.

"For our citizenship is in heaven, from which we also eagerly wait for the Savior, the Lord Jesus Christ,"
- Philippians 3:20

"Surely I am coming quickly."- Revelation 22:20

C.- Count it all joy.

"My brethren, count it all joy when you fall into various trials..." - James 1:2

"Though now you do not see Him, yet believing, you rejoice with joy inexpressible and full of glory,"
- 1 Peter 1:8

E.- Encourage one another. We need fellowship.

"Let us consider how to stimulate one another to love and good deeds, not forsaking our own assembling together, as is the habit of some, but encouraging one another; and all the more as you see the day drawing near."
- Hebrews 10:24-25

God bless you as you continue to walk with Him in joy.